MW00641846

Out our way

Out our way

gay and lesbian life in the country

michael riordon

between the lines

© Michael Riordon, 1996

Published by
Between The Lines
720 Bathurst Street, Suite 404
Toronto, Ontario M5S 2R4
Canada

Ordering information for individual copies see last page.

Cover painting, Mulet Country, March, by Eric Riordon (1904–1948)
Cover and interior design by David Vereschagin, Quadrat Communications
Backcover photo by Brian Woods
Printed in Canada

All rights reserved. No part of this publication may be reproduced, stored in a retrieval system, or transmitted in any form by any means, electronic, mechanical, photocopying, recording, or otherwise, except as may be expressly permitted in writing by the publisher, or CANCOPY, (photo-copying only), 6 Adelaide Street East, Suite 900, Toronto, Ontario, M5C 1H6.

Between The Lines gratefully acknowledges financial assistance from the Canada Council, the Ontario Arts Council, and the Canadian Heritage Ministry.

Canadian Cataloguing in Publication Data

Riordon, Michael, 1944–

Out our way : gay and lesbian life in the country

ISBN 1-896357-05-9
1. Homosexuality – Canada.   2. Gays – Canada.
3. Lesbians – Canada.   4. Country life – Canada.
5. Sociology, Rural – Canada.   I. Title.

HQ76.3.C3R56 1996   305.9'0664'0971   C96-930136-7

For Brian

CONTENTS

VI Over the rainbow, somewhere

PREFACE

NINE YEARS AGO MY PARTNER AND I LEFT THE CITY.
Along with a truck-load of stuff, our dog and our cat, we lugged with
us a lifetime of second-hand terrors about Life in The Country. We'd
seen *Deliverance*. We were two gay men. With no contacts and hardly
any money. On a dirt road up a hill in the middle of nowhere. In a
ruin of a house with no toilet, no bath, the outhouse overflowing, the
well nearly dry, and winter looming. We had the same questions then
as other city folks still do: Aren't you scared out there? Don't you get
lonely? How do you make your living? Are you out of your *mind?* It's
to answer such questions that I've written this book.

When mainstream culture notices gay and lesbian folk, it tends
to see us as urban. And our own media-makers have their hands full
transmitting the stories of lesbian and gay downtowners. But more
and more of us are choosing to live wherever it suits us. This is a free
country, no? And as one gay man in northern Ontario said, "It's my
goddamn country too." It's for us that I've written this book.

We hear an awful lot of loose, foolish talk about The Gay
Lifestyle, The Homosexual Agenda, and Family Values. Some of it
comes from deranged people who are actively bent on doing us harm,
but much of it from people who just don't know any better. It's for
them I've written this book.

The way I see it, people in power stay in power first of all by
commanding our attention. Kings, CEOs, and other overdressed des-
pots would collapse in a moment without our awe to prop them up.

They trick us into believing that what they do or say is infinitely more compelling and significant than anything the rest of us might do or say. Oh, yeah? Not in my book.

Sometimes folks who live in the city – as I did four-fifths of my life so far – forget there's anything out here but scenery. The view is a little different from the middle of nowhere. While the city may be the place to get a lifestyle, out here is where life actually begins, and ends. If small farms die, watch for more square tomatoes that taste like yesterday's news. If the oceans die, and the forests, you and I are worm food. So it's for all us living things that I've written this book.

What counts as rural? A lesbian from a Newfoundland outport calls Cornerbrook "the city" – it's got a mall. Her partner laughs; she grew up in Chicago. By rural I mean not-the-big-city, I mean places where we lack the critical mass of our urban cousins, so we have to do things differently. Like locating a reliable source of porn, or Birkenstocks.

To find people for the book I put out a paperstorm of notices, letters, and ads in gay, lesbian, and mainstream publications across Canada. Many well-connected folks helped out by suggesting contacts I'd never have reached otherwise, and these led willy-nilly to many more. In all I met about 300 gay men and lesbians. I travelled on and off for a year, some 27,000 kilometres, by car, bus, train, and various-sized boats and planes. Like Blanche Dubois, I depended greatly on the kindness of strangers.

To produce a book of affordable length, I had to put aside, with regret, many stories as rich as the ones included here. In addition, places and people I didn't reach could fill many more volumes. That includes much of Québec. I have neither the skill nor the resources to do extensive translation of intimate conversation. When a group of lesbians and gay men in Rouyn-Noranda spoke with Brian and me in their own first language, it was a quick, sharp lesson in how francophones must feel in most parts of Canada. To the First Nations and francophone people who shared their stories in what for them was a second language, many thanks.

You'll find very few people of colour in this book, alas. By and large, rural areas are about as welcoming to them as to homos, only we can hide better than they can. Also absent are city dwellers who grew up rural. Since that takes in about sixty percent of the Canadian population, I decided early to limit my search to folks who are currently living in the country. I've also chosen not to pursue people who define themselves as bisexual. Some women and men in the book *are* bisexual, but felt it important to identify as lesbian or gay. After all, the only part of the *bi*sexual that's under siege from our enemies is the *homo*sexual, yes?

Where participants have chosen to conceal names or places to protect the innocent, I've put pseudonyms in double quotes the first time they appear.

Without the Canada Council and the Ontario Arts Council, I could not have made the search this book required, nor afforded the time to write it. The knives are out for the arts councils. They need and deserve any public support they can get.

Warm thanks to Martha Gould for editing with insight and respect, and to Marg Anne Morrison at Between The Lines for her warm, enthusiastic support of this project. And finally, I'm deeply grateful to all the folks I met for their courage in revealing so much of their private lives to a voyeur with a tape recorder.

A young man met me at the bus in northern Alberta. Since he lives deep in the closet with his Jehovah's Witness parents, we'd agreed it would be best if I stayed at a motel. Instead, he took me home to stay with the family. "But," I asked, "how did you explain me?" "No problem," said he, "I told them you were writing a book about gardening."

By then we'd pulled into the drive and there was Mom, waving. Over dinner they asked me what I knew about gardening. "Nothing really," I said breezily, "that's why I'm writing the book, to see what I can learn. And by the way, it's not really about gardening." I caught a glint of panic in my young host's eye. Served him right. "It's actually about – *northern* gardening." How well we learn to embroider a lie.

When I left, Mom and Dad came out to say goodbye. "We'll be sure to look for your book," Dad called. What could I say? "You do that," I called back. "Just look under vegetables and fruits!"

I always knew I was different

▶ 1   PARTICULAR FRIENDSHIPS

NORTH BAY, ONTARIO, DECEMBER 1969. NORMA IS TEND-
ing bar in the lounge at the Golden Dragons Restaurant. It's packed.
Next door Ruby, her brother, Ronny, and their band are pounding out
dance tunes for a Christmas party. Ronny nags his sister to go talk to
the bartender. "Ronny could always spot which one was and which
one wasn't – you know, gay," Ruby recalls. Ronny himself was, and is.
Ruby had a look at the bartender. Don't like her, she reported back to
Ronny, she's not my type.

Nearly three decades later, in the small house that Ruby and
Norma share, we're flipping through snapshots: Ruby and Ronny
grinning in their rock & roll gear, Ruby's grandchildren – seven so far,
and her first great-grandchild. Warm April sun floods the living room.
Norma and Ruby live half an hour's drive from North Bay, beside a
birch-lined lake. Ruby is sixty; Norma, fifty-seven.

Ruby's dad was a logger in the northern bush. Her mother bore eleven children, and cooked for a couple of dozen men. "We didn't have electricity or anything like that," says Ruby. "But I never heard her complain, not once." Her dad used to call Ruby his right-hand man. He taught her to fish, to guide, to find healing herbs in the woods, and to run the logs. "I'd do it for the tourists, you know, jumping from log to log? Never could swim, until one time I nearly drowned." She was seven.

Ruby was never too keen on being A Girl. "Every time they tried to put a dress on me, I'd rip it up or flush it down the toilet." By this time they had indoor plumbing. Even so, at sixteen it was decided she would be married; it was all arranged. "Marriage was the last thing I wanted. Before the wedding I was all set to run away with Donna, my girlfriend; we had the whole thing planned. But my mother wouldn't let me out of her sight." The marriage lasted twenty-one years, and produced three children.

In the early '60s, Ruby and Ronny sneaked off to see a doctor in Rouyn, across the border in Québec. Each of them underwent a battery of tests, to see if they could be changed, to become like everyone else. The doctor offered Ronny a startling option: if it would help, he could become a woman. He declined. For Ruby nothing could be done; she would just have to get on with her life as is. She cried a little, then did as he said.

Norma grew up a city girl in the United States. As far back as she can remember she'd had "these feelings, these deep feelings for other girls – I didn't know what they meant, and I certainly didn't know what to do about them." She longed to get away. Two escape routes beckoned – the military, and the convent. At nineteen she moved to Montreal, entered a convent, and for ten years devoted herself to a teaching mission in the Philippines.

In the convent she found herself in deepening relationships with other nuns. "They were emotional," she recalls, "not physical." Even so, Mother Superior did her best to nip them in the bud, these dangerous "particular friendships," as they were called. "Then two of my relationships became physical. In the middle of the night I'd be sneaking around on the back stairs." In the morning she would confess that she'd been indulging in "excessive familiarities." To her great surprise, the father confessor seemed not at all surprised. A few Hail Marys and she was up the back stairs again.

It sounds so comical now, the mischief, the *sacrilege*. But for Norma, it was torture. "I took my vows seriously, but I was doing these *things* – the only word I knew for myself was 'sinner.'" In the Philippines she was sent to a priest-psychiatrist. Desperate, she came out to him, and with a fine regard for both professional and confessional ethics, he turned her in to the Mother Superior. "By then I had to get out anyway, I felt so bad. I really believed there was something terribly wrong with me. I thought I was the only one, you see, and I was corrupting those other nuns." Norma left the convent in 1969.

With another ex-nun, a former girlfriend, she formed a small band to play dinner music. They headed north and landed a job playing at the Golden Dragons Restaurant in North Bay. In no time the other woman was gone, yearning for the big city and a man. Norma stayed on, tending bar at the Golden Dragons. And then Ruby walked in. Apparently her first impression of Norma didn't last.

"The first time we had sex," says Norma, "I felt *so* guilty. After the nuns, now here I was corrupting a married woman!" Ruby ended the marriage, told each of her three kids – two were still at home – and moved into an apartment with Norma. There were rocky times with the young, some awkwardness at a daughter's wedding, but it all smoothed out in time. In 1973 the two of them exchanged rings. Their witness got drunk, and slept through the whole thing.

From the late '50s Ruby had been driving a city bus; she was the first woman transit driver in North Bay. Some of the men tried to give her a hard time, but she cut them short. "I've got kids to feed, just like you." She says it as fiercely now as in the moment. "And I've got just as much right to this job as any of you." End of discussion.

Eventually Norma got work on the buses too. By then surely people must have known; North Bay isn't that big, even now. "Well," says Norma, "you'd be surprised. Some of them will say things about gays right in front of me, so that makes me think they don't know."

"We don't hide," Ruby adds. "Most of them know we live together."
As a co-worker puts it, they keep house together. They plan to build
an extra bedroom onto their house, for Norma's mother and her
boyfriend when they visit from Florida, or any of Ruby's brood.

Six years ago, Ruby was diagnosed with breast cancer. Last year
she suffered a relapse, bone cancer this time, lost all her hair to radia-
tion treatment, and came very close to dying. "They were good with
us at the Sudbury hospital," says Norma. "No one ever tried to block
me from being with her. And now it's me her kids ask if she's really
okay, or just pretending." A little short of steam, Ruby had to quit
work. But she's gained weight, and her hair has grown back – not
brown like before, but jet black. She assigns her new gift of life to an
herbal remedy called Essiac, developed sixty years ago by a nurse not
far from here.

"Hey," says Norma, "tell him about the wolves." Ruby used to
play baseball in the nearest town, then she'd have to hike a mile and a
half back home to the logging camp, through the bush, at night. "The
wolves would be howling on both sides of me. Next day you'd see
their tracks, right there by the trail." Wasn't she afraid? "Nope. My
dad told me they wouldn't hurt me. They will never hurt you, he said.
I used to think of them as dogs; I'd call back to them. And they never
did hurt me."

2   LOCAL HERO

AFTER SUPPER ONE WARM SUMMER EVENING, JIM
stepped out for a walk with his boyfriend. They followed the road that
snakes along the bay, out past the fish plant. The boyfriend put his
arm round Jim's shoulders, as people do. "Well, you wouldn't believe
it," says Jim. "Down there by the plant they gawked, they whispered, a
few of them even started shouting at us. Then along comes this truck.
The driver stares at us, he can't take his eyes off us, and before you
know it the damn fool drives straight into the ditch and turns his
truck wheels-up! Of course he jumps out and starts cursing us up and

down, 'What the hell do you think you're doing?' By now this big crowd has gathered. 'Staying on the road,' I told him right back, 'which is more than I can say for you!' The crowd laughed their heads off; they loved it. Me too; I laughed so hard I almost died." He laughs now, a warm, soft laugh. "I think we gained a little ground that night."

Jim Genge has lived all his forty-eight years right here in Glovertown, Newfoundland, at the south end of a long bay that winds out to the Atlantic. Population, 2,200; main industry, fish processing. We're sitting by one of the plants now, looking out over darkening water. The three plants here are in trouble – in some recent years the capelin (a kind of smelt) never even showed up.

Jim's roots run deep here. His grandfather and father were boatbuilders, and he operates a cottage-size sawmill across the road from his house. He has people cutting trees for him – black spruce, balsam fir, juniper – and with one employee he cuts them into boards. He's just got an order from a builder; it'll keep him busy for a couple of weeks.

By his teens Jim knew he was gay. "I was attracted to every Tom, Dick and Harry – well, mostly the dicks." He chuckles merrily. His face is remarkably smooth for his age, and what he's endured. "It really hurt being in the closet so long. Once I started drinking, I got to doing it an awful lot." At thirty-two he married. "At the same time I happened to be going with her brother. On our wedding night she caught the two of us hard at it. Threw one of my boots at my head, nearly killed me!" Another laugh rolls out of him. The bride held on for a year, then walked. "There were no kids, thank God. Just one big dog." The brother married, the dog died, and Jim drank.

The boyfriend with whom he upset that truck went off to St John's and didn't return. Others came and went, most of them married. An eight-year affair with one local man ended abruptly when "a ladyfriend walked into my house – like a damn fool I forgot to lock the door, and we had music on. Unfortunately she has a big mouth, so in a few days half the town heard about it. Some I considered friends haven't spoken to me since – mostly the pentecostals. They weren't really friends, I guess." The man refused to see him again.

By this time Jim was getting pretty sick of his own small world.

He sent away for a flood of gay literature from Halifax, anything he could get his hands on. Isolated too long, now he corresponds with support groups in St John's and Cornerbrook, but hasn't got to a meeting yet – it's a three hours' drive by the Trans-Canada to St John's, and four to Cornerbrook. He writes to cabinet ministers in Ottawa and St John's, badgering them to include sexual orientation in their human rights codes.

Now and then he fires off a letter to the Halifax-based *Gaezette* (a gay and lesbian paper, now called *Wayves*), describing his situation here. From the responses, he's garnered enough pen-pals from Canada and the U.S. to occupy most of his evenings. His P.O. box runneth over.

Then he took on the booze. Uncomfortable in the local, very straight AA group, he sent away for advice on starting his own. "It only takes two to start a group, and I already knew one other here, so that's what we did. We just did it ourselves."

Armed with material from the gay and lesbian church in Halifax, he came out to his pentecostal parents next door. His father said nothing at all, and his mother managed only, "It's your life, Jim." One brother and sister, pentecostals both, have shunned him. "I really don't give a shit what they think. I've got a pretty thick skin by now. And I'm proud of who I am. Nobody can take that away from me, not anymore. Besides, we have a saying round here – if you can't make nothing of a man, at least you can make a pentecostal of him. So there you go."

Jim Genge wants out. "This is a small, narrow-minded town. I want to live in the city, to be around other gay people. But there's no work I can do there." On the other hand, business isn't exactly booming here; he can't be putting much by. "I want to take a course in saw repair at Fredericton. Anywhere there's a mill, they need maintenance. I could travel around and do that."

But now it's getting late; he has to go home. He has a date tonight. From the next town, the guy is married, has an adopted kid, and a wife who knows what he's up to. "So you share him then," I say. "Well, yes, I suppose. But when he goes home, I'll be alone again, won't I."

Most of what he's done here, he's done alone. When he escapes, he may well have to go it alone out there. But if Jim Genge does get his wish, a ticket to the gay city shimmering just over the rainbow, I suspect this particular small, narrow-minded town won't have a clue how much it's lost.

3 AUTUMN, THE FIRST

SEPTEMBER 1, 1986, WE CHUGGED UP THE HILL IN A rented truck almost as big as the house. The dog was peeing, the cat vomiting. With a lesbian friend from the city we set about making the place ours. This was not a question of lifestyle, but of shit in the stairwell, piss in the closets, fire damage in the wall, and decades of rubble everywhere. The house was known as a poor house; why would anyone take care of it when it could never be theirs?

Soon the leaves were falling, the nights frosty, and Diane had to go home. Now and henceforth it would be just the four of us – Brian, Michael, Smudge the dog, and Willy the cat. Dear God, what had we done?

I was born in Montreal, a war baby. My first few years I lived on a mountain top in the Laurentians, rambling the woods and meadows with my older brother and a Shetland sheepdog. Then my father, a landscape painter just making a name for himself, died of cancer. (That's one of his later paintings on the cover.) I was four. In 1949 my shattered mother moved us to Montreal, and went off to work in a department store. Her mother, my grandmother, swept into our lives to play mother. Isabel was an autocrat of the old school; she ought to have been running an army, not a house with small children in it. But we were all she had. The world was ours, she taught us, it was there to claim.

It's hard to say when I realized I was gay, I tried so very hard not to be. Did the right thing, dated through high school and a brief, silly career at university. But always I had one special friend, a boy, usually another lonely boy that my family would call a loser. I remember two

English teachers in high school, both extravagantly effeminate and known to live together. There was a cruel, unspoken conspiracy to drive them mad, or out, and I was one of its leaders. Perhaps I knew their weak points. I recall maddening Mr McDonald into throwing a Bible at me. I won much acclaim that day.

For me to have had *sex* with another boy, or even a girl, was inconceivable. Instead I fell for the Saturday afternoon TV wrestlers – not the beefy Russians but the exquisitely sculpted good guys. All right, it wasn't love so much as lust, but how was I to know they weren't the same thing? For years, my trysts with these rough-and-tumble lovers would be my only sexual outlet, and my awful secret.

If the world was mine, why did I never feel I belonged in it?

In 1968, a year before the historic Stonewall riots in New York, I read in *Time* magazine that an American psychiatrist was curing homosexuals with electric shocks. Still not admitting even to myself that I actually *was* one, I moved to Toronto and signed up with a former student of this mad Pavlovian scientist. Twice a week for one year he shocked me while I watched slides he'd collected of muscle men. By that time I had a girlfriend, the proof of a cure. Our attempts at sex – for her needful, for me dutiful – were embarrassing to both of us.

We soldiered bravely on for a year. Then I sold everything and got on a ship bound for Europe and North Africa, to find myself. It was and wasn't the right place to look. I steered clear of countless opportunities for sex with men, but finally managed to write my mother from Tunisia, telling her I was gay. In Athens I witnessed, quite by accident, the brutal suppression of the first student demon-stration against the military dictatorship. Suddenly, overwhelmingly, I saw precisely what was wrong with the world. A handful of tyrants and their hired thugs were determined to keep the rest of us from being free. Until that day, I hadn't noticed I was anything but.

Back in Toronto, I read every book I could find on any sort of liberation struggle – except my own. After several months of this, I bullied myself into calling a gay help-line, and ventured out to the steambaths. I carried with me, perhaps for protection, *The Collected Plays of Bertolt Brecht*, volume 2. I was thirty. Soon I joined the newly formed Gay Alliance Toward Equality, and in no time became its Education Coordinator. We organized, leafletted, marched – the same few faces at every protest – and raged at the legions of our cohorts hiding away in the bars. I churned out fierce and funny articles for *The Body Politic*, a gay and lesbian journal that died in the '80s. We really did think we could remake the world.

Working at a gay dance, I ran into the shrink who'd tortured me – he was gay too, after all, and by now he'd turned his attention to smoking and fear of flying. By this time I'd got the knack of sex, but never quite managed the evangelical pursuit of it that came to be required of proper gay militants. The effect of the shocks was to make me fear my own desires, probably a pre-existing tendency in an inheritor of abuse. Nevertheless, I lived for a couple of years with a lover – we did everything wrong, could have written a textbook. Then in 1981, at thirty-seven, I met Brian. He was thirty-two.

A fan of my work in *The Body Politic*, he asked for an introduction via one of his housemates, with whom I'd been working on a new phoneline for gay and lesbian youth. Gathering his nerve, Brian invited me to supper. We talked through most of the night, then I left to go home. In the grey pre-dawn I looked back. He was standing on the verandah, smiling, so beautiful. I was filled – no, *flooded* – with something I'd never felt before, a great surge of warmth, or joy, or – well, I suppose it was love. Two weeks later I asked him to supper. That night I jumped him.

Brian had always dreamed of living in the country. For me hiking and canoeing were fine, but *living out there* I could hardly imagine. On drives to hiking trails, we'd remark on this place or that – too big, too small, too close to the neighbours and so on – but it was all comfortably abstract, out of reach, a one-of-these-days kind of fantasy. Brian worked in a small cabinet-making shop, and I was a free-lance writer; we had hardly enough resources between us to buy a shed. Then one day in Prince Edward County we saw an agent's name on a For Sale sign. On a whim, Brian called her. Within a couple of weeks she had shown us a dozen properties, all well out of range, even in fantasy. The last place on her list was a run-down one-and-a-half storey house on a dirt road, with sixty acres of woods, up the steepest hill in the county. Four grand old maples lined the drive. They were asking $30,000.

So here we are, the first autumn. We've put in a woodstove and bought a load of wood – it will be our only source of heat. We've patched the roof, covered the windows with plastic, dug out the outhouse, cleared the immediate yard of major debris, cleaned and covered up the worst interior horrors with paint. Autumn rains have filled up the well. Home sweet home.

That year the first snow fell in October. The silence was terrifying.

▶ 4   BEHIND CLOSED DOORS

AS NEARLY ALL OF US ARE, "JEAN" WAS RAISED HETEROsexual. "On the other hand," she says, "I've always admired strong women, the ones who are what they are, who don't knuckle under to the rules. My mother was like that. She had to be to raise six kids on her own." Jean herself didn't marry, but did have sex with men. "I went through the motions. But I never felt what you were supposed to. I never felt much of anything with a man." At eighteen she got pregnant by a fellow who played in a band. "I really didn't want this guy in my life, so I never told him about the baby." Seven years later her second son was born in similar circumstances.

Jean is thirty-six. She and her two boys live on the edge of a village – gas station, general store, a few short streets – about an hour's drive from a small city in northern Ontario. Their vinyl-sided bungalow overlooks stubbly field and bare woods beyond. It's early March. The drapes are closed. Her small grey furball of a dog jumps onto my lap, falls asleep. The boys are at school.

At twenty-nine, needing better-paid work, Jean took a two-year course in early childhood education at the community college in town. And fell in love with one of her professors. "I couldn't believe it; I didn't know what hit me. I was scared out of my wits that people would see what I was like when I was around her. I'd do anything just so she'd notice me." By the second year "Clare" had noticed. Teacher and student entered into an emotional relationship, very gingerly, a first for both of them. "I thought I'd died and gone to heaven. Finally love felt like it was supposed to."

As soon as Jean graduated, Clare invited her to come live with her on the small farm where she bred horses. "I'd been raised to believe this kind of thing was absolutely taboo. But there was no way I could deny any more what I felt." She and the boys moved in. Clare had one other housemate, "a really nice lady," says Jean. Each boy would have his own room, and Jean would bunk in with Clare.

One night after the boys were in bed, the two of them watched *Desert Hearts*, the movie version of Jane Rule's classic novel of lesbian love. "When those two women kissed, it was *amazing* – it was *so scary!*" A back rub was offered, and nervously accepted. "By this time I could hardly breathe. I was sure I wouldn't know what on earth I was supposed to do. But it just happened, you know? It was so natural, so easy, like this is how it was always meant to be. The first two years of the relationship were the best in my life."

But soon the questions began. Jean's mother wanted to know why she was sharing a room with this other woman. It was the only bedroom left, Jean explained. Then why don't you just put the two boys together? Because they need their own space. Jean got better at eluding questions as she went. For their part, the boys took to the new place in no time; they especially loved the horses. "But I couldn't tell them anything about us; I didn't dare. It was so uncomfortable; we couldn't touch each other, we could hardly look at each other except behind closed doors." The housemate never said a word.

They had no relatives, no friends they could tell. "I really hated that, not being able to tell a soul about this relationship that was so important to me. You get awfully good at hiding your feelings." At their jobs, she and Clare would carefully avoid making any reference to the other. "I wasn't afraid so much for myself as for how they might treat my kids if it got out. So I started doing things in public to separate me even more from Clare. I'd be very critical and sarcastic. I really hurt her."

At home the tension mounted. "With all this pressure building and no outlets, we were fighting more and more, and getting into a lot of emotional abuse." Her voice is wavering now, her face turned a little from me. "After a while it started to get physical. One time she hit me, and it burst my eardrum. That was it. We had to separate." Jean is crying now. I stop the tape. All I can offer are platitudes, so I just wait. The little dog raises his woolly head, watches her. She excuses herself, makes some tea, and we resume.

These days Jean is making moves. She's come out to her older son "Martin," and he seems to have taken it in stride. She hasn't told the nine-year-old "David" yet, but says, "He's such a warm, caring person, I can't see how it will be a problem. He already believes men and women are equal, which is pretty amazing." Even so, she remains cautious. "People talk. And kids can be so cruel. I know things have been said to Martin about his mum being a lesbian. What's he supposed to do with that?"

Jean has bought herself a few lesbian books and videos by mail, but they're expensive for a single mom, an RNA on casual contract with no benefits. She subscribed to the Toronto lesbian paper *Quota* until it shut down. And she finally got up her nerve to venture into the public library in town. "I did find a couple of books there, but I felt so awkward, I signed them out under a false name, and had a friend take them back." She's not out to anyone at work, not yet. "Generally if I hear anti-gay stuff, I'll let it pass, but if it really gets my back up – usually it's about AIDS – then I'll say something. It's the least I can do."

And what about Clare, is she history? "No, we've actually started seeing each other again. We work hard at the relationship now, very hard." Clare's farm is a couple of miles down the road. The two of them ride, go to horse shows, drive to work together – Clare to the college, Jean to the hospital. And Clare comes over Saturday nights.

"We're much more cautious with each other now. You can't

erase what happened. But there's too much love there just to let it go. I don't know what will come of it. I really don't."

5   THE STORMS, MY GOD

HIS BED AND BREAKFAST WAS A FISHERMAN'S HOUSE, AT the mouth of a coastal river in Nova Scotia. When he moved in five years ago, Ken had picture windows put in, the pond dug out, and a low grassy dune levelled to open up the view. There it is, the Atlantic. It's calm today, but in another month the first of the winter storms will come howling in.

Seventy-two years; it's a long story. Ken grew up in a small southwest Ontario town, joined the air force at eighteen near the end of the war, serving on the east coast. Loved the climate, made a note to come back some day. "I did notice that I liked the male body, the male person. What would you expect, living on a base with 1,500 men?"

After the war he returned to Ontario, to university, and married. "Everyone was doing it then; it was the only thing to do." A year into it he caught his wife in bed with another man. "I should've got out right then, but for some stupid reason I stuck it out." Twenty-three years later the marriage collapsed, bitterly. "In all that time I never horsed around, not once, not with a man or a woman. I believe a relationship has to be monogamous, or else what's the point?" He talks of it as if it had just happened; it still smarts. They had three children.

For thirty years Ken worked as an accountant. "And I hate figures, I can't stand 'em," he says. He lived for a while in Toronto – "awful place, I'd never want to go back there" – then in New Liskeard, a mining town in northern Ontario. Then, tired of the isolation, he got a transfer to London. At a party he met a teacher; they clicked. "I thought I had the world by the tail. That man was the first real love of my life, the gay friend I'd been looking for." They bought this house on the Atlantic, they had big plans for it. Then the friend walked, and left Ken holding the mortgage. "I hate to say it, but I think I was just a meal ticket for him."

Ken placed a want ad in a Halifax paper. One of the replies came from a young man. "He was twenty-seven, good-looking, a terrific lover, and he cared for me – grey-haired, sixty-eight-year-old me. I couldn't believe my luck." They saw a lot of each other, travelled south to Ken's house in the Carolinas. The young man was always broke, so Ken paid the bills. Then one day the local Mounties showed up at his door. They were looking for the young man; he was wanted for theft. Only then did Ken notice that some of his cheques had gone missing.

He sounds weary. "I seem to keep making the same mistake with people. Loneliness will do that to you; it makes you vulnerable, and people take advantage. I'd just as soon be alone. I don't like it, I resent it like hell, but...." He looks out the window. Two tiny figures cross the shiny dark tidal mud flats out there, stooping now and then. "They're after the clams," says Ken.

Warm days like this, he and Mike will wander the mud flats at low tide, gathering the succulent mollusks. Mike is a seven-year-old Airedale of deep voice and noble bearing. He goes everywhere with Ken. "Mike is my best friend."

Ken's neighbours have all accepted him, he says. But they don't really know who he is. "Whenever any discussion comes up about being gay or homosexual, I don't say I'm for or agin, I just let them talk it out, then I change the subject." Isn't that painful? "Of course it is. But what are you going to do? As soon as straight people know you're gay, watch out. They'll accept you up to the fence, but they'll never let you open the gate."

Old friends of his are dying, not of AIDS but Alzheimer's, or heart. "It makes me feel so vulnerable. I love this place, and I don't want to go into an apartment in town, but I could die out here and who would know? Only Mike." In actual fact, one time when he was too tired to answer the phone, a gay friend down the coast drove twenty-three miles up here to check on him. Periodically Ken will visit this man and his lover, another gay couple who own an inn, or a friend who also lives within a few hours' drive. They help fill the gaps, he says. "But when you say goodbye there's no one to come home to, no one but the dog. I just want a friend. I don't even care all that much about the sex any more. All I want is a good friend." He's not whining, just speaking his heart.

Outside, Mike's bark signals intruders – no, they're guests, two pairs of mothers and daughters out for a weekend by the sea. Ken bustles about, takes bags, directs them to their rooms, apologizing that they're not made up yet, and warns them about the bath – old pipes, no pressure. They check out the view. He tells them about the ducks and geese he used to keep on the pond, but either a coyote or a bobcat got them, every last one of them. And the storms, my God....

▶ 6   NO LIFE LIKE IT

IN HIS LATE TWENTIES, RESTLESS AND UNHAPPY IN southern British Columbia, Brendan saw a want ad in the *Buy & Sell* newspaper: "Farmer in the Charlottes seeks ..." He'd always wanted to live on a farm. He headed north and out to sea. His beloved horse, Comanche, would follow six months later.

The farmer is Tim Reid. By his teens in eastern Ontario, he knew he was different. "The thought of dating women was totally alien to me; I had nothing in common with them. I figured that join-ing the military would straighten me out." At eighteen he signed up with the navy. This was to be his career, his life. But the straightening out didn't happen quite as he'd hoped. "Like many others I'd go off the base and do my thing. I figured as long as I stayed away from mil-itary personnel there wouldn't be any problem."

In 1979 he started to notice he was being followed off the base, and his phone was making strange noises. "I was in communications, so I could tell it was being tapped. I thought, okay, standing orders said you had to report any known homosexuals, so I went in to my commanding officer and reported myself." Shortly after, he was taken into custody. "They wanted to know the names of other gays. I would never turn anybody else in. I was forced to take drugs – the base doc-tor said they were tranquilizers – and then they interrogated me, for three or four days. They called me a traitor, a disgrace to my country. They made me look at pictures to identify which men I'd slept with. When I refused to answer, I was beaten, all over – wrapped up in a blanket so it wouldn't show – and injected with what I now believe to be scopolamine. It's a drug that lowers your resistance to answering questions. After that it gets kind of fuzzy. When I came out of it I was under house arrest; then I was discharged." On his papers they stamped "Not Advantageously Employable." He can never work for the military again, nor in any civil service job that requires security clearance. "Oh yeah, and they outed me to my parents. You can imagine how that went over." Tim was twenty-one. He was ordered never to speak of these events.

With a man he'd met, Tim took off to the Yukon. They rented some land and tried to raise goats, sheep, and poultry. When neither farm nor relationship proved viable, Tim loaded the remaining animals onto his truck and headed south. His ark came ashore finally in the Queen Charlotte Islands, eight hours by ferry off the B.C. coast. Nearly broke, he wintered in a cabin on the beach, battered by icy Pacific gales. Then he bought a trailer, and placed his want ad in the *Buy & Sell*, "Farmer in the Charlottes seeks ..."

Tim and Brendan bought four acres of forest, cleared three of them with chainsaw and hired bulldozer, trucked in two old cabins, and joined them to make a house. It's a work in progress, their home, held up by rough yellow cedar posts and faith. In winter storms they fear for their roof.

The place is walled in by tall trees, and overhead looms a heavy sky, raining as usual in the spring. Moss and mildew grow luxuriantly – on walls, in closets, on clothes and furniture. They can't keep hay dry for the horse. But the sky also provides all their water; they collect it off the roof in huge barrels. They grow and raise as much of their food as they can; on an island where virtually everything but fish is imported, prices are astronomical.

Tim is thirty-eight now; Brendan, thirty-one. Tim's logging job died when cutting ended on native lands in the Charlottes. Like many other ex-loggers out here, Tim is bitter about the first inhabitants.

"They don't pay taxes, they get these huge houses for nothing, and then they cost the rest of us our jobs." Income is a sore point. Brendan is sick of cooking at the hotel in Masset; Tim hasn't been able to find any other work. And it's not about to get better. The major source of revenue in the area, the military base, is due to close.

What about sex out here, are they monogamous? It's nosy, I admit, but I've journeyed to this outer edge of Canada to investigate how we make out – in every way – in the rurals. Silence. They glance at each other. Then Brendan says, "Yes, we're monogamous – or else." "Another sore point," says Tim. "It was only once." Brendan looks grim. "Well, if it happens again...." They leave it at that, and so do I.

Mid-way through supper – one of their chickens, roasted – Tim leaves the table without a word, opens the back door and CRACK! a rifle shot; I nearly hit the ceiling. "A bear," he says, sets the rifle by the door and sits again. Bears often wander into the yard. "Usually it's enough to fire into the air," says Tim. "We'd only shoot them if they attacked the animals." Brendan is furious. "Are you crazy? You can't just go firing off guns without warning people!" They skirmish; supper resumes.

There seems so little comfort here, only work to be done. They get off the island once or twice a year, if that – it's a major expedition. They had one gay friend, a teacher who's since left the island, and a few heterosexual friends with whom they'll have supper now and then. "You know," says Brendan, "isolation is probably the only thing that keeps us together. If we were living in the city, we would have split by now for sure." Tim: "As soon as we can find a buyer for this place, I expect we'll go our separate ways." They've been told that under their topsoil lies a rich store of gravel. It's not exactly diamonds, but any resource that doesn't have to be hauled in by boat is a prize around here. So having struggled so hard to make this place a home, they'd sell it as a gravel pit? "In a second," says Tim. Then Brendan is off to work at the hotel.

Tim smokes non-stop, and takes medications for depression, anxiety, and ulcers. The military nightmare isn't over for him, far from it. In 1986 he broke his silence to testify before a federal commission on human rights. Since then he's been fighting for an apology from the military, and the reinstatement of his security clearance. One Minister of National Defence after another has turned down his requests. The latest, David Collenette, wrote: "You were treated in accordance with the regulations in effect at the time of your service.... There is unfortunately nothing further that can be added concerning your case." Not only in Somalia, it seems. Tim and Brendan have received phone calls threatening both their animals and themselves. "But I won't back down. If it's the last thing I do, I'm going to get this thing rectified."

If he got his security clearance back, what would he do? Tim: "I want my job back in the military." Michael: "You're kidding." Tim: "Not at all. That's all I really want." Michael: "But *why?*" Tim: "My issue is with the security unit, not the military. I love the military; I always have. I want to get in there and fix it, make it okay to be gay or lesbian. It's legal now, but that doesn't mean it's okay. I want to change that." Michael: "Well, good luck." Tim: "I know it's going to be tough. But that's what I'm going to do."

▶ 7   LIFE LINES

FIVE RINGS, A TAPE CLICKS, A COOL, PLEASANT MALE voice comes on. "Hi, and welcome to Gay Support. This is a confidential phone line which offers support to gay, lesbian, and bisexual men and women in Newfoundland. We realize that calling us may be a frightening or intimidating experience for some of you. We know how you feel, because we've all been there."

The voice belongs to "Philip," and he has indeed been there. From age five, he knew he was different. An outsider at school, he was acutely aware of boys in an uneasy way but didn't know why. He took up music, he says, "for self-preservation as much as anything." Later he would develop close friendships with women, but froze when he encountered their sexual desire. His own found expression only with the glossy men he met in skin magazines picked up on visits to

Toronto. In 1977 he moved to Newfoundland, to teach classics and music at the new college in Cornerbrook. When a composer friend came out to him, he was stunned and terrified.

Not long after his father killed himself, Philip's mother fell sick. "She simply gave up. I was so angry with her for that. She died without my ever telling her that I loved her. I was damned if I'd ever let that happen again." Telling it now, he cries. Finally in 1991, in Ottawa for the performance of two newly commissioned pieces, he came out to a gay friend. He was forty-three.

On the west coast, Cornerbrook is Newfoundland's second largest city, spiked by a thick plume of smoke from the pulp mill that dominates its core. "Sometimes I'd love to be in a bigger place, one with a good-sized gay community." A holiday in San Francisco left him goggle-eyed. "Everywhere I went – clubs, restaurants, stores, on the *street* – I got this overwhelming sense that being gay is normal. I felt totally relaxed; it was an amazing confidence-booster."

Back to Cornerbrook. "It's a mill town, a sports town; there was no culture to speak of here. Even around the college, you tend not to get invited to things if you're single." He decided he had two choices: he could seek out greener pastures, or he could make a life for himself where he is. He enjoys teaching, but knows at forty-eight it wouldn't be easy to find another job – "By now I'm too expensive." In seven years he can retire. So here he is, making a life for himself.

He joined the board of the local theatre company, a motorcycle group, and the AIDS committee. But the project that commands most of Philip's energy is BGLAS – Bisexual, Gay and Lesbian Association for Support. "When I joined a few years ago, there was only a handful of us, and no focus really. We decided the best way to draw in more people was to start a phoneline. People are so isolated in all the little towns and outports up and down the coast. By phone you can make contact and still be as anonymous as you like."

The line opened in 1995, advertised in the local paper and on TV. Staffed by volunteers, men and women, it's open for three hours one night a week. Very soon they were getting up to eighty calls a week, from all over Newfoundland (it's the only such line in the province), and even a few from Nova Scotia. When the line's not open the machine stays on, and Philip's voice reminds callers, "The only thing we ask is that you not use our phone line as a date line." And what if they do? "Knowing how hard it can be to make contact in the first place," says Philip, "we don't want to shut anyone out. Instead we'll try to get at what might be behind the call; more often than not it's loneliness. People are desperate to know they're not alone out there. Of course you want to solve everybody's problems, but you can't. We just try to get them to keep talking, listen carefully, ask questions, get them to maybe look at things a little differently."

"Morrissey" lives with his parents in a small town up the coast from Cornerbrook. He's seventeen. We made contact by phone; he was at a friend's house where he could speak more freely. His parents, he says, are very conservative. "My sister asked them what they'd do if it turned out I was gay. 'We'd disown him.' That's what they said." His sister is a lesbian, lives in St John's, and is out to practically everyone in the world but her parents.

"I always knew I was different," says Morrissey. It keeps coming up. Different how? "I always knew I liked boys. By the time I got to high school I was pretty depressed about it. I kept to myself; I got to be very anti-social." How did he spend his time? "Reading. That was about it." Didn't date, play the game? "I tried really hard to think about girls – you know, fantasies – but my mind would always turn back to boys. I thought about suicide a few times, but I didn't have the nerve to do it."

Wasn't there anyone he could talk to at school? "Forget it. I was way too scared to tell anyone, especially an adult." Someone his own age then. "If you heard anything about gays at school, mostly it was the 'Take 'em out and shoot 'em' type of thing."

In Cornerbrook for a workshop at the college, Morrissey happened to see a notice on an office door – Philip's office – giving the number of a support line. He learned it by heart. "Finally one night I got the chance to call when my parents went out for a drive. It was great, I could talk about anything – what I was going through, this girl I know who was with a guy I really liked – she's bisexual – anything."

He became a regular caller. "Talking to someone made me feel much better about myself. I finally started to see that it's not weird to be gay, it's just – normal. I can't imagine what I would've done without the line."

"One of our success stories," says Philip, proud as any parent. And all this with virtually no funds. What about the miracle worker on this end of the line, what does he want? He hesitates. "I want to finish a chamber piece that I've been composing for ages. It has a gay theme, and I think it'll be very good – if I can ever finish it. And of course I want somebody to love. I'm not interested in one-night flings; they just don't do it for me. I'm not naive, and I'm well aware that I qualify now as an older man. But my life so far has been built on coincidences that've been thrown my way, so I've pretty well given up trying to predict what'll happen next. One thing I am sure of though – my soul will know when it recognizes a kindred." "Oh," he adds, "and I have a real fetish for straight hair. Not curly, has to be straight. It drives me wild."

▶ 8   CRUISING THE INTERNET

"A RELATIONSHIP I WAS IN HAD JUST ENDED, AND I WAS sort of depressed about it," says Renée. "This friend said, 'Come on over to the computer lab and we'll get on the IRC.'" For techno-peasants like me, that's Internet Relay Chat. Renée continues, "I'm like, oh no, I won't know what to do, I'm computer illiterate. He said it's not a problem – they talk, you talk, it's cool. So he gets on this channel called Happy, where there's no particular topic, people just chat. I scroll down through the list and there's this *lesbian* channel – I'm like, oh wow, this is cool."

Renée Steeves is twenty-one. She lives with her parents near Wolfville, in Nova Scotia's Annapolis Valley. Renée always knew she was different, she had serious crushes on other girls. When puberty hit, she finally put a name to it: lesbian. She managed to avoid heterosexual entanglements, tending instead to be a loner. A year ago she told her parents. "It was a really huge relief, like not having to lie any more." She made herself over into what she calls Superdyke. "I was pretty scary – chains, leather, the whole thing – really butch. It was kind of a backlash, I guess, I'd been repressing for so long."

She's kept the Doc Martins, black shirt, and jeans, but shed the hardware. "Now I define myself by who I am, not by what anyone else expects of me." She took off to Toronto for a course in music recording. The tuition cleaned her out of funds, so she came home, and works in a fast food place in town. "Can't afford to leave home again. But that's okay, my family and me are pretty good friends now." A few of her other friends are gay, the rest straight. "I don't choose them by sexuality, but mostly by other interests we share, like music."

Having discovered the lesbian channel, Renée dove in. "I wasn't working at the time, so I just hung out at the computer lab for hours and hours." Several people I met on my travels told me if you're out in the middle of nowhere, the information highway is the only way to get around. Technically, most any place with a phone line has access. Still, it's easier said than done. Computers aren't exactly standard items in most rural households, and long distance charges put casual cruising out of reach for many of us. Until recently, students (and friends, on the sly) could use the Acadia University computers in Wolfville quite freely; some would while away whole nights hooked on the Internet. In time the authorities took note, and now access is restricted.

A wide-eyed tourist, Renée was amazed at what she found out there. "People would send you messages saying, like, do you want to have Net sex? I'm like ughh, that's really creepy, it was like a meat market." She left that channel, wandered awhile, and found the Nice Cafe. "It's a virtual coffee house. You drink a cappuccino, you talk about the weather – you know, it's just a friendly kind of place to go." She dropped in regularly. "I became friends with this one particular person; we talked for weeks and weeks. After a while I found out she was female. So I asked, like, are you involved with anybody? 'I'm a lesbian,' she said. Oh my God, so am I!"

The other woman attended the University of Arizona. The two

of them started sending e-mail back and forth. Then "snail mail," actual letters with stamps on them. Then phone calls. They traded photos. Then clothes. Term ended, and the other woman came east for the summer in Detroit – half the distance to Nova Scotia. One night she called to say she'd have to go home soon, to California. "I told my mother I had to go to Toronto. She's like, well why? To see some friends I met last year. Okay, so – when? Tomorrow. I could see she knew something was up, so I told her about this girl on the computer. She thought I was completely crazy."

Renée caught the next flight out of Halifax, her cyber-friend the overnight bus from Detroit. "I knew all the places to go in Toronto. We spent this totally crazy, fantastic week together. Then I came home, got into a huge depression, and I haven't been on the IRC since." Why not? "You'd think that it would be hard to fall for someone over a computer. But after talking to them for hours and hours and hours, it's surprisingly easy. Maybe it's just me, but I fell, really fast. Now she's there, I'm here, and I miss her."

But that's life, isn't it, you can't really blame the computer. "It's just not real," says Renée. "It's very romantic; it paints a picture of something you really want to have but you never can. The whole thing was like a fantastical, magical fairy tale." So she wouldn't go tripping through cyberland again? "Never. I hate it."

Famous last words, if you ask me.

▶ 9   GWM SEEKS

WE HURTLE THROUGH SPRING-GREEN ROLLING HILLS. On the dusty dash a sign proclaims: "I love being exactly who I am," with a lambda, the chosen gay sign. A gopher scurries onto the road – thump, under the tire it goes. We zoom on. "I treated a woman last week who swerved to avoid one of them," the driver explains. "She went off the road, she was a mess." "Desmond O'Ryan" is a doctor in rural Alberta. All his moves are quick and assured.

We turn down a winding lane cut through poplars and spruce,

into a clearing at the centre of his quarter section (160 acres). "I built here because I don't want any neighbours spying on me. I can even pee off the porch, no problem." The clearing is dominated by two connected angular black domes – Desmond's house, covered for now in tar paper, but he plans to seal it with liquid rubber. A friend calls it Madonna's Bra. Down a long corridor cut out for hydro poles, the land slopes away to foothills, and snow-peaked Rockies beyond.

His dad was a lay pastor, then taught at a two-room school in southern Alberta. At four the boy started crossing the road to school – it was a handy substitute for daycare. Later, in a more structured school, he was younger and smaller than his classmates. "I was a pipsqueak really, I never fit in," he recalls, "so I had to do most things on my own." Also around age four he started searching encyclopedias for images of naked men, classical statues and the like. "I was fascinated by male genitals. Even the Jolly Green Giant," he grins. "I kept wondering *what* is under that tunic?"

In due course he discovered porn, stealing it from corner stores. "Only fags paid for it – *I* was a thief!" It had been drilled into him that fags go to hell. He prayed that he'd get over it, burned the porn and quit masturbating – several times. Then on April 7, 1980, he had what he calls his conversion experience. He found – well, stole – *The Gay Mystique*, a myth-breaking book for many. That's it, said Desmond, I'm gay. He was twenty-two. But still he didn't fit. The men he met wanted to hang around in smokey bars. He wanted to hike, ski, tumble down wild rivers. To pay his way through medical school he worked in lumber camps and did an eight-year stint in the army.

Now he's a part-time physician, mostly filling in for others on leave. "I don't want to get lost in it – it's my work, not my life. And if you get settled in a practice, people start asking too many questions, and you have to tell lies." He's not out then, hence the lyrical pseudonym. "Let's say I'm on the way. I'm writing this article on homosexuality under my own name, for the medical association magazine. I really want to educate my fellow physicians a bit, to correct some of the more bizarre misconceptions about us. In my work I see all kinds of disgusting things that heterosexuals have done – wife-beating, child abuse – and I know very well that if any of *us* had done these things, they'd be blamed on our homosexuality!"

This part of the world is not famous for its tolerance of minorities; Aryan Nation and KKK organizers find fertile soil here. "I don't have any doubt that the Nazi thing could happen again," says Desmond. "There are times I can actually imagine waking up to pounding on the door in the middle of the night. Of course I hope I'm wrong, but if the right wing keeps marching on the way it's doing...."

Yet here he stays, alone. There have been lovers. The most recent decided to become a woman. "To tell you the truth, recently I've started doing the ad routine." He laughs, a little embarrassed. He shouldn't be, I assure him, I've met a number of men in fairly remote places (no women, as it happens) who swear by the classifieds. Each one of them reported disasters, misfits, false starts and such, but when was it otherwise in human affairs? Some found lovers, others good friends.

Desmond advertises in the city papers, gay and straight, and in the occasional newsletters of the Rural Gay Men's Group, an informal contact network currently based on Vancouver Island. His ad reads, "Rural GWM, mid-30s, good-looking, who's maxing out on life intellectually, emotionally, physically, creatively, and spiritually, is keen to meet a similar type dude who is willing and able to meet the challenges of a relationship, to meet its rewards."

How does he do? "I get responses, especially from the city. Some of them are dillies; you wouldn't believe them. I write back to a few, tell them a little more about me, my interests, my philosophy of relationships and so on, and I ask them to do the same. I've even gone so far as to meet a few guys, but none of them have really shivered my timbers. Next time I'm going to ask them to name their favourite TV shows. If they have a whole bunch I'll know they haven't got a life."

What is his "philosophy of relationships?" "The problem is," he says, "it's in flux right now. I used to feel my life wouldn't be complete until I had a lover, until 'the other half of me' arrived. Now I'm very content with my life as it is, by myself. Maybe I'm just turning into a crotchety old son of a bitch." Yet still he puts out ads – why? "I suppose I still have fantasies of finding an all-out companion, a running mate. But if that individual fails to show, do I sit around moping or do I take life's gifts as they come, in different people? If that's the path I'm being led down, well, okay, fine."

Some of life's gifts lie scattered around Desmond's forest clearing: the truck with camper mounted, the half-made shed a pottery-to-be, a vegetable and flower garden with rows of early sprouts, a compost toilet turned into an impressive flower pot (never did work right as a toilet, he says), Madonna's Bra still under construction, a pair of sleek kayaks, one for white water and one for the ocean, a mountain bike, skis, an old organ, a synthesizer, an Amnesty International bulletin, scribbled notes for that article he's writing. "I do have a few things going here," he laughs. "Once in a while something will even get finished."

▶ 10 CIRCLES

BY NINE THE LIGHT IS FADING, BUT EVER SO SLOWLY. MY host explains, "At this time of year, sunset isn't an event, it's a process." It's early June in Yellowknife, capital of the Northwest Territories, population, 14,000 or so.

We make our way to the barbeque by canoe, gliding along the rim of the bay past a jumble of small houses. Building materials cost the earth here, so the inhabitants recycle, scavenge, make do in a riot of giddily expressive ways. As a backdrop, several standard-issue grey office blocks rise up from the downtown core. We duck under a low bridge, swing round the seaplane dock to land at the modest bungalow that Shauna Yeomans shares with her partner, Chris. It's years since I've been to a party, and I'm nervous as a debutante.

Three quarters of the crowd are women. Shauna sits comfortably in a loose circle that includes her mother, up for a visit from Alberta. I ask Shauna for subtitles; who *are* all these people? She laughs. "My friends are quite diverse. At an event like this the circles tend to overlap." She points out a small group, a little noisier than the rest. "They're the jocks – I used to be really active in women's sports. And those are the granola lesbians. Just look for the Birkenstocks. Then there are the heterosexuals I've gotten to know over the years, mostly couples. This is a small enough place that you get to cross a lot of different paths. I like that. In my experience almost everyone has something to offer."

Shauna's lived half her forty-two years here. She grew up on a farm in Alberta. She knew nothing about homosexuality, but found herself developing strong emotional attachments to other girls and women. But lacking any positive information or role models, she coasted along in denial. At nineteen she slept with another woman, both of them protesting that they were really heterosexual.

To earn some quick cash for a trip to Europe, the two of them got government jobs in Cambridge Bay, Northwest Territories. "It's so far north we couldn't even find it on the map." The sexual relationship didn't work out, the other woman being a fervent Roman Catholic who eventually married and had kids. Shauna dated men both in Cambridge Bay and when she moved to another job in Inuvik. "Mostly it was for appearances," she says. "I also had an affair with the woman next door, at the same time that her boyfriend and I were best friends!" The two women moved to Yellowknife, Shauna into another government job, but they split up when the other one went with a man. "Finally I decided enough is enough, okay, I'm a lesbian."

Several people described Shauna to me as the lesbian mother hen of Yellowknife. She laughs. "A lot of people come and go here. I've been around so long, I guess I've been there for quite a few younger lesbians who were coming out. I've sort of taken them under my wing until they got into their first relationship, and I've been there for most of the break-ups, too."

In other towns or cities of this size, I've heard of a seasonal exchange of partners among lesbians, what one woman called "spring cleaning." Another joked, "We don't have one-night stands like those dirty men; we have three-month stands." Shauna responds, "That's not limited to small places, it's a fact of life. I was in Winnipeg for a while, and it's exactly the same. In fact with this place being so small and tight-knit, people here have to think twice about the consequences of their actions. Relationships take time to get going, they take time to heal, and you've got to deal with the baggage."

It's after one. The party's still humming, but so are the bugs — this time of year they're bloodthirsty. My host and I paddle out from Shauna's, swing round a rocky island, past a flotilla of home-made houseboats, across the bay and home. I can't get over it; we can still *see*. I've heard of this phenomenon, but the actual effect is stunning, a slow bleeding of soft light from the sky. For people who live here it's a signal to get outside and stay there, until they're forced in again by the gathering darkness and cold.

Does Shauna ever get cabin fever, does she ever long for the bright city lights? "I used to like going to the clubs in the city, but now I really don't give a shit. I'm just happy to get home again." This is it then, home, for the foreseeable future? "Well, my ideal, my fantasy would be to spend the summers here, and head south for the winters. I'd love to start up a retirement home for gays — especially for the ones who aren't in relationships. We could use something like that, don't you think?"

Once a mother hen....

▶ 11 DANS NOTRE MONDE

MANON: "THE PARTIES ARE A CHANCE TO BE WITH YOUR own people for a change. Here *we're* the ones who are normal!" Stéphane: "You can relax, because for once you don't have to explain anything to anyone." Marie-Paule: "It's a place where you know you belong." Diane: "It's not just cruising here. You get more chance to talk to people than at a bar." Louise: "It's like a big family." Paul: "Aux partys nous sommes dans notre monde." At the parties we're in our own world.

We're sitting in the smokey kitchen of Diane Toupie-Grégoire in Rouyn-Noranda, a small city in northwest Québec. Toupie is her nickname. She's the president of Action Gaie Abitibi-Témisca-mingue (AGAT), and six others here are members. Then there are the anglos, Brian and me. Two mining towns amalgamated to form Rouyn-Noranda, with a combined population of about 40,000. Half a block from Diane's place, a large copper smelter fills the night sky with a smudgy glow.

Marie-Paule Rivest is forty. Born in a village at the south end of the region, she came to Rouyn-Noranda at eighteen for a course, and works as secretary in a local high school. "I like the city," she says, "I'd never go back to my village." Marie-Paule had her first sexual experience with a woman at seventeen. "I also went with men, but by my late twenties I knew I felt more complete with a woman – it was *so* much better!" Everyone laughs.

Marie-Paule's partner, Manon Désalliers, is twenty-nine. She was born in Val d'Or, another mining town to the east. She drives a school bus. "From about ten I knew I was attracted to girls, but I thought I was the only one like that. In my teens I played baseball, and there I started to meet girls who were lesbians. When I was eighteen my father caught me in bed with my girlfriend [ma blonde] – we made too much noise! He gave me a big speech, you won't have any future, blah, blah blah. It doesn't bother me if people don't approve of me. I'm gay, that's it, that's all." She has an uncle who's gay, and a younger brother. "I'm making a trail for him."

Thirty-six, Paul Fortin is vice-president of AGAT. He grew up in Kamouraska, a small town on the south shore of the St Lawrence River, and came to Rouyn for a job in nursing administration. He lives in the village of Macamic, an hour's drive to the north. "I was always attracted to boys, both emotionally and physically." He had his first homosexual experience at sixteen, then lived a couple of years with a woman. But from age twenty-five, he decided to be who he was. "I told my six brothers that if they didn't accept me, I wouldn't see them again. They accepted me. I don't hide at work. Heterosexuals can live as they wish, and so will I."

Louise Hogan, Diane's partner, grew up here in Rouyn. Forty-one, she's a federal civil servant. "When I was quite young I told my mother I wasn't interested in playing with dolls; I prefered my brothers' trucks." But until her mid-twenties she went with men. Then she went to a gay bar in the city with a friend, and there she met her first girlfriend. "I hadn't said anything to my family, but one Christmas Eve my present girlfriend [Diane] told my sister about us. They're okay with it, except for one brother. He invited me to visit him in Ottawa, but he said Diane wasn't welcome. Of course I didn't go. We don't really talk to each other now. My mother doesn't know officially, but she knows – Diane is always welcome at our place."

Diane was born here. She's forty-three. At eighteen her mother found her in bed with a girlfriend. "She asked me if it's what I really want. I said yes, I think it is." She'd also been out with boys. "But with a girl it always seemed more equal, more balanced." When she went out with a girl under eighteen, someone reported to her parents that she was after young girls. Her father hadn't known she was gay. "It was hard for him – I'm the only girl." Diane moved to another town to be with her lover, "la femme de ma vie." When the relationship and her job ended, she came back to Rouyn. Now she works as a technical consultant in a truck garage and body shop. She's come out to some of her co-workers, but not to others. "When I hear them talk about queers and fags, forget it. You have to know who you can trust."

Marco is twenty-five. He works in the restaurant at the local arena. From age fourteen he was aware of being turned on by boys, about eighty percent, he says, and twenty percent by girls. "But I was very hidden; I only ever had sex away from here, at my friend's place in North Bay." He was in the air cadets, and homosexuality was definitely taboo. At twenty-two he decided it was time he lived for himself. Came out to his family, no problem. No problem at work. "My boss happens to be my mother. Stéphane comes with me to social activities, and no one says anything. If someone doesn't like it, I'm not going to lose any sleep over it." He and Stéphane became lovers two years ago.

Stéphane is twenty-eight. Born here, he had close relationships with boys from about age five, and sex from twelve. "I've always been homosexual; I've never slept with a woman." Marie-Paule: "You don't know what you've missed!" Paul: "I envy you!" The remarks fly like this for a moment. In his mid-teens Stéphane started going to the disco in a Rouyn hotel, which is ostensibly straight. "I met gays there, and finally I knew I wasn't the only one. But after sex I'd feel disgusted, full of shame, afraid of anyone knowing."

At nineteen he went away to college in Montréal. His mother and two brothers came to visit, discovered Stéphane and his boyfriend [mon chum] living together in one bedroom, with one bed. After the intial shocked confusion, his mother asked if he was happy. Yes, he said, I am. After three years in the big city, he came home. "As they say, you can take the boy out of Abitibi, but you can't take Abitibi out of the boy." Now Stéphane's brothers call Marco their brother-in-law. "As long as my family accepts me I'm okay. I don't go around announcing myself as Stéphane, homosexual, but if anyone asks I won't deny it." Recently he's gone back to school, to study special education.

Until 1992 in Rouyn-Noranda, people would meet at the hotel disco or at private parties. These were occasional, tending toward the exclusive, expensive, and a lot of work to organize. Then a few people decided to establish an organization for the whole region. They called it l'Association (now Action) Gaie Abitibi-Témiscamingue, wrote themselves a charter, and registered with the government, compulsory in Québec since the group charges membership fees and derives income from its dances. In three years it's become the largest gay and lesbian group in Québec outside the major urban centres.

In a poll, the majority of members said they wanted a mixed group that would welcome both women and men. Stéphane: "It's a huge region, and one of the least populated in Québec. A group for men or women alone couldn't survive here." Diane: "In the city we discriminate against each other, but not here." A majority of women said they prefered *gaie*, with the feminine *e* added, over *lesbian*. Diane: "Some women even said they wouldn't join if we used the word lesbian in our name. Some of us hear the word in the same way that gay men hear *fag* or *fairy* [*tapette, fifi*]."

To join AGAT costs only ten dollars a year. A ticket to a dance costs members three dollars, non-members six. These dances are famous across the north, even in Ontario – people will drive several hours to get here. The crowd averages about 150. Diane: "One man in his sixties told me he was married but gay, where could he go, surely he was too old for the dances. I told him, Non monsieur, we have people from eighteen to seventy-five." The latter is Marie-Paule's father. He came out at sixty-two.

A local hotel provides the ballroom free of charge. When one of the hotel managers objected to having all those homos on his premises, Diane announced immediately that she was seeking another location. "The management practically begged us to stay. From their cut of the drinks plus the rooms they rent to people from out of town, they make close to $3,000 per dance. And it's eight times a year."

The group advertises in the local paper, at the university, and in several gay publications in Montréal. Paul: "Some people think they still have to go to the city if they're gay, so we want them to know we're here." Aside from the dances, AGAT also organizes public meetings, one, for example, with a lawyer experienced in human rights legislation, and several on HIV and AIDS. The group has good connections at the local health and social services centre (CLSC), the SOS suicide phoneline, and the health department responsible for people with HIV and AIDS. Diane: "Because it's a remote region here, there's a tradition of people helping each other. If we know a doctor who takes gay patients, we'll tell the CLSC. And they will refer people to us who are lonely and isolated."

The people gathered in Diane's kitchen are obviously proud of what they've built here. Stéphane: "People in the city think it's backward up here; they ask if we have electricity yet. But for me it's easier to be gay in Rouyn than in Montréal. There you can only be gay in the ghetto." Manon: "We don't need a village or a street or even a bar of our own [a recent poll turned down the idea of gay bar here], we just belong." Diane: "Of course we don't provoke people. I don't kiss my girlfriend in front of my family. We touch, but we're respectful." Manon: "We want the same respect that we give to them, that's all."

Paul: "It's harder to be single here than in the city, that's for sure. Between parties it's not easy to meet people." Diane: "On the other hand if you're in a couple it's easier here; people aren't so quick to go after your girlfriend."

Recently a member announced the location of the upcoming dance on the radio. Security was doubled at the hall, but there were no incidents. Diane: "I don't care if they say it's at the usual place, but I don't want the location to be named. There are still people around with closed minds who could do us harm." Paul: "But we have to come out of our cocoon more. There are so many of us out there who are still alone, in the closet." Diane: "Of course we need to reach out more, but I don't want anyone in my gay family endangered because of that." Paul: "Unless you already know what it means, AGAT doesn't say anything. We should be using the word gay more." Diane: "That's fine with me. All I'm saying is...."

It's late, and we have another long drive tomorrow. We leave them like this, in Diane's kitchen, working out the future of their ever-extending gaie northern family.

12 GIVING BIRTH

"THERE ARE NO BARS AROUND HERE," SAYS K. "NO PLACE where you can really be yourself and hope to come out of it in one piece."

"Here" is a rural town called – believe it or not – Bible Hill, near Truro in northern Nova Scotia. A chilly October rain brings down the last of the leaves in the yard. K continues, "There was no safe place where people could make contact. So me and another lesbian decided to do something about it. First we had to find out what people wanted." They advertised a public meeting, rented a room, and to their amazement over sixty people showed up, spilling down the stairs. "The excitement was so high that night," says K's partner L, "no one wanted to go home." And thus was CNGML born – Central Nova Gay Men and Lesbians.

As young girls K and L both sang in the same small town church choir, a few miles from where they live now. Though K remembers strong attractions to women teachers at school, she married, became a Catholic, and kept her desires well in check. But by the time she was twenty-five the charade had collapsed, and she came out to her husband. "We're still friends," she says. "I always got along well with men, like with my best girlfriends' boyfriends – we tend to share the same interests, especially hunting and fishing." After a spell of depression, and a brief encounter with a psychiatrist who was only interested in pushing pills, she met, or rather re-met, L.

L grew up with four brothers, hung around with their buddies, and never thought of herself much as A Girl. "Nor did I ever let myself think anything at all about homosexuality. I grew up with a pretty black-and-white view of morality." For a while, alcohol helped keep the feelings at bay. Then she got into sports, which led to more and more female contact – the pressure kept building. Then at a party a woman kissed her, on the lips. "Finally I had to admit there was really something there, and I knew it was what I wanted. I was terrified." She was twenty-five. Shortly after that, she and K became friends, and then lovers. "It was rocky for a while," says L, "But here we are."

L is thirty-seven; K, thirty-five. K: "Ever since I can remember I always wanted to marry, settle down, and have kids. It just never occurred to me that you could do that with a woman!" They bought their house from K's gay brother, and K tried to get pregnant. For two years they kept trying, driving twice a month to a doctor in Halifax, at $175 a visit. When they could no longer afford these trips – K's a warranty clerk for a truck company, L a free-lance bookkeeper – they tried fresh sperm, donated by two gay friends. Finally this year, K gave up. "It was getting much too stressful and depressing to keep on trying."

At that first meeting of Central Nova Gay Men and Lesbians, everyone wanted something different. The core group decided they'd try to organize a cultural or social event every second month, and a dance every other month. Their debut event drew over a hundred people – in a freezing rain storm. K: "It showed how hungry people were. They'll drive four, five hours to get here; they'll even come from Halifax and Moncton where they've got their own groups and clubs." L: "Our events are different from a bar; they're friendlier, less like a meat market." Now CNGML rents the Lions Club hall, and hires a straight DJ, with none of the hassles they expected. But the group still runs on a shoestring, hanging on from event to event – speakers, a film, bowling, a camping weekend.

K and L have applied to adopt, but they aren't holding their breath. "A lot has to change in this province before that's ever going to happen." If L can find a regular job with benefits, she may try the pregnancy route.

In the meantime, they continue to take care of their other baby. The small group that started CNGML intended that others would be running it within a year. They're still at it. As usual, people are quick to criticize, but much slower to lend a hand. Some men don't want women at the dances, and vice versa. The music's too loud or not right, the group is too public or not public enough. "At the last dance," says K, "this woman was complaining to me, why didn't we have more dances, more events. I asked if she'd be willing to help out, and just like that – she disappeared."

L: "Sometimes you get fed up, you think why am I putting up with all this nonsense, who needs it."

K: "But then it always comes back to the same question – if we don't do it, who else will?"

II

The gay lifestyle

▶ 13 WINTER

I HEAR WOLVES HOWLING, NOT CLOSE BUT NOT THAT far either. The treetops clash in a fierce, cold wind. I'm warmly dressed, flushed from skiing, but feel a sudden chill. These woods are haunted. Last winter an elderly woman went out for a walk from her house down the road. She froze to death, here, in these woods. I wonder if that was her plan. It wouldn't be such a bad way to go.

The first winter. Some days we can't get up the hill. After an ice storm we can't even get down, not alive. Upstairs there's no insulation; we could be living in a tent. We go to bed with our clothes on, heavy socks, and tuques. Mornings we have a choice: go down in the teeth-chattering cold, make a fire, and sit wrapped in blankets waiting to get warm again, or stay in bed and be found in the spring. The pipes freeze, and the drain. Of the sixty house plants we brought from the city, eleven survive.

Each morning before it's light, Brian goes off to work for a local contractor. I send out reams of work proposals to cultural gatekeepers in the city. Like notes in bottles from a desert island, they disappear over the horizon, and then – nothing. All day I talk to myself – what am I doing here, what day is this (as if it really mattered), who the hell am I? By the time my loved one gets home, armed to the teeth after working all day with a gang of straight men, I'm wild-eyed and babbling. But we remind ourselves that we love each other, and we remind each other why we're here. Then the pipes freeze, again.

Growing up in eastend Toronto, Brian was fooling around with other boys by the time he was eight, experiencing little shame – that would come later – and an intensity that seemed somehow different from that of his partners. He made brief detours into heterosexuality, but continued to prefer sex with men. At nineteen he went away to university. "That was the darkest time for me, when I had to face the fact that I was going to be gay for the rest of my life, but still didn't want to be." By now he was fully aware of society's rules, and where he stood as a homosexual. He dropped out, tried suicide, did drugs, and drank. Alcohol fueled the cruising, lubricated the encounters, and kept the terror at bay.

At the same time, Brian also trained and worked as a medical lab technologist. In 1971, hungry for change and fired by a vague, passionate sense that things weren't right in the world, he volunteered with CUSO in western Africa, supervising a hospital laboratory and teaching lab technology. A stranger in a foreign land, he was very cautious about sexual contact, and in the end had none. He came home determined that never again would he deny himself in such a fundamental way. In Montreal to study microbiology, he joined the collective that ran Androgyny, a downtown gay/lesbian/feminist bookstore. "The personal is political" was a governing principle of the day. To Brian that meant coming out, and coming out meant being who he was, without props, despite the terror. In 1980 he quit drinking.

Now everything was open to question. Turning away from a budding career in science, he returned to Toronto and studied wood-

working. He moved into a house with several other gay men, support-
ing himself as a waiter and daycare worker. With the Reagan/
Mulroney dark ages descending, he helped start GLARE, Gays and
Lesbian Against the Right Everywhere. Then he met me.

And here we are. We've moved from being quite out to being
quite discrete. It's an odd sensation, like starting over from scratch.
The neighbours who help us haul our firewood – by now we cut our
own, which is butch enough without having to lug the stuff too –
know us as a couple, or as good as. But we never actually say The
Word.

As an Amnesty International letter writer, I know that every day
in most of the world people are seized, bundled into cars, tortured
and "disappeared." To be out in any way, to express the faintest desire
for freedom – sometimes even to *think* it – can be fatal. I'm ashamed
of my own fear, here in what's still a remarkably sheltered, safe place
for most of us. But fear is fear, and shame doesn't help.

Years ago, before Brian or any fantasies of country life, my first
radio play was broadcast on the CBC. It told of two gay men living on
a farm, Hallowe'en, harassment then outright attacks by unseen
neighbours, a night of terror. But that was fiction.

We've chosen a place deliberately out of sight from any neighbours' view. Like most choices, this one has a downside. Another winter, late night. Suddenly, a loud knock at the back door. They've come
quietly; the dog didn't hear a thing. Hardly breathing, I half open the
dark-paned door. You can't not open in the country, not in the winter.
Two men, no coats. "Our car is stuck in the ice back there. We need to
call a tow truck." I know the spot; they could be telling the truth. I
invite them in, indicate the phone. At least one of them smells of
liquor. "Our friends, they're freezing out there." There are *more* of
them? The big knife, is it in the drain rack? I admit two more men,
grey with cold. "We thought you might be scared if all of us showed
up at once." As if we aren't now. I make coffee, they thaw, we chat
until the tow truck comes. Then they're gone. "They were gay," says
Brian. "For sure," says Michael. Then why didn't we say something,
anything? Why didn't they? Such are the habits of fear.

Now Brian has his own workshop; we built it ourselves. He works alone, makes fine furniture on commission, and never knows when – or *if* – the next job will come. Neither do I; I'm still sending out notes in bottles. With our Canada being so quickly broken up and the parts all sold, with our earth being plundered to extinction, who but bankers, those corporate loan sharks, can count on anything? We balance on tiny grains of sand – quicksand. Another winter night. I go outside to pee. It's perfectly still, perfectly quiet. The snow sparkles. In the deep black, diamond-littered sky I can see every single star that ever spun across the heavens.

Ah yes. Now and then I have to remind myself. This is why we're here.

▶ 14 VIEW FROM THE EDGE

DAVID SQUINTS INTO A DAZZLING EARLY SUMMER SKY. After several years of withering drought in south Saskatchewan, last year it rained so much the wheat roots rotted in the ground. "It's not hard to see why people quit farming," he says. But he carries on, with 720 acres in wheat and barley, mustard (for the oil), beef cattle, turkeys, and chickens.

Behind us are the barn, tractor shed, chicken house, and grain bins on one side of the yard, David's beloved flower garden and weathered house on the other. His great-grandfather built the house in 1906. At the moment things are a bit chaotic; David's partner, Doug, has just moved in. Doug works as a physiotherapist in Regina, forty-five minutes to the south in good weather. They drive in together when they can – to make ends meet, David has to work at a gardening centre in the city.

David is forty-four. Until he was thirteen his family had no indoor plumbing – it was his job to carry out the "honey buckets" in the morning. He inherited this land when he was twenty, quit university, and has been farming ever since. His brother lives a stone's throw down the drive.

"I always knew I was different," he says. "But all I ever heard about homosexuality was either jokes or horror stories, so I kept it all bottled up." Under heavy pressure to marry, "I just withdrew, didn't have a sex life worth mentioning. I was really depressed and suicidal in my early twenties." Then he started going into the city, met people, found a lover. "That relationship was a mess," he says. "Neither of us had a clue how to talk things out. He was a coke and booze addict, and I got into some of that too. We both ended up in twelve-step programs." And broke up. "There I was, isolated again. Maybe it's just age, but I really found the club had got too wild for me." Still, it was there he met Doug.

Now thirty-eight, Doug emigrated from England in 1981. He'd been attracted to people of both sexes, but after three years of marriage, "It dawned on me that I was actually happier with men." Making the switch was no great hardship, he says. Maybe it's his job, but Doug radiates calm. "Our first six months were hard," says David, "I was still running away from my problems, and I was very hyper." Doug smiles. "Both of us have given a lot of ground since then." For him the adjustment to country living is just beginning. "It's so small here, a stranger really stands out. But I'm getting used to it. Now at least I can go into the post office and ask for my own mail!"

To expand their social circle, they tried to organize a network of gay couples, but it never gelled. "It's amazing," says Doug. "The same people who say wouldn't it be nice to spend a weekend in the country will drive five hours to a bar in Calgary, but not forty-five minutes to get here." David: "Some of them panic if they get out of sight of a mall." A smile plays just below the surface with him; I've noticed it often in the short time I've been here. "Well, you've got to laugh," he says, "either that or go nuts. It's something about the view from the edge."

In this case the edge is a mixed farm on the prairies at the end of the century. "I haven't earned enough in a decade to pay any income tax," says David. Out here 720 acres counts as a small farm, and small farms are an endangered species. "This place is too big to work without machines, but too small for most of the machines you can get.

And with the extremes of climate we've been getting, in the past few years we must've lost half to two-thirds of our topsoil."

David tried keeping goats, but he was a little too far from the city to deliver the milk. To grow vegetables or fruit on any scale he'd have to irrigate, and for that he'd need a more reliable source of water than an uncertain well. He tried growing herbs, but the summers were too short, the temperatures too volatile. He talked to the local co-op about marketing raspberries, but "I was about twenty years too late, everyone's doing it now. That's the trouble with trends. With so many of us scrambling to survive, people will jump at anything, borage oil, llamas, ostriches – I mean, how many feather boas can the world actually use?"

The end result is unrelenting stress. Some gay lifestyle. Why does he keep at it? "We're peasants; I'm rooted here. I still have my great-grandfather's bill of sale for the place – he's buried a quarter mile from here. And I can't imagine starting over – at my age? What would I do – get a face lift and work the streets?" The smile surfaces, like sun through a cloud.

"There are compensations. Suddenly I'll be aware of a perfectly calm day in the field, or the smell of fresh-cut hay. Or I'll have a sense of accomplishment when the grain bins are full – even if they're not worth a whole lot. And my flower garden is very important to me." It shows. In mid-June, still early on the prairie, already it's a lively play of colour. I notice two large, oddly shaped planters. David chuckles. "They're old ceramic urinals; originally we got them for the pigs' water. They're so heavy the pigs couldn't tip them over."

Doug arrives home from work in the city. "This relationship is what I wanted twenty years ago," says David, "but I stopped believing it would ever happen." Doug replies, "He's not too quick about some things, but I think he's starting to catch on that the feeling is mutual. That's the thing with gay relationships out here – there really aren't any scripts available, so we have to improvise."

"I guess all we can hope for now," says David, the smile about to erupt, "is that the Chinese develop a taste for beef."

▶ 15 THE FUTURE

"LYLE" GREETS ME AT THE BARN DOOR, IN OVERALLS and carrying a cell phone. A biting wind sweeps the yard. This is one of the coldest Januarys on record.

We sit in his basement office. Every few moments he glances at a computer screen. His broker calls. "What do I do," Lyle asks into the phone, "give it to the eighty-seven-and-a-half area?" Now he's transfixed by the screen, which is dancing with numbers. He taps, taps, taps a pen on his desk. It's a nerve-wracking business, farming.

Lyle grew up here; he took first grade in the one-room school across the road. Went off to agricultural college, "more to get away from home than anything else," but when his dad's health failed in 1978, he took over the 260-acre farm. He was nineteen. Since then he's expanded the operation to 1,100 acres, 700 in soybeans, 200 in winter wheat, another 200 in corn to feed the beef cattle he raises. Lyle is thirty-seven.

I ask him about growing up gay, but he's very distracted. There are the numbers on the screen. And each time we hear a creak from upstairs, he pops out nervously to see if anyone's coming – his parents share the house with him. I return to the subject of farming; he relaxes. What's the computer for? "I keep track of the soybean numbers from the big U.S. markets." Soybeans aren't covered by a marketing board in Canada, so Lyle can sell his crop when and where he likes. "I produce about $300,000 a year, so if I can make even five percent more by good marketing, it's well worth my time."

The broker calls again; they commiserate over the continuing good weather in Brazil. This is futures trading, a vast electronic gambling casino. The game is to buy what amounts to *a contract to buy* a given quantity of some commodity at some given future date, then to sell that contract at a higher price than you bought it. Lyle has bought a bundle of soybean futures. Good weather in Brazil means a good crop, and a good crop can mean lower prices, which at this point is not good for Lyle. The stakes are high. "When they had those big floods in the U.S., beans went up a dollar and a half in four weeks. If you played your cards right you could easily have doubled or even tripled your investment in a month. Of course it can go either way, which is why it's such a tricky game."

The market doesn't close for another few hours, and for the moment the price of beans has levelled out. I suggest we go for a drive. Lyle looks relieved. The car whumps through snow drifts, on roads that run flat and straight to the white horizon. Now we can talk. By the time he was fourteen he knew he was different, and by sixteen that he wasn't likely to change. Even so, when his male friends started marrying in their twenties, "I got real serious about dating women. That was the most miserable time of my life; I couldn't wait until those dates were over." Stir-crazy by age thirty, "I figured I had to at least find out what's out there."

He answered an ad in the London paper. "It was a disaster. He was the wrong type of individual entirely for me, very effeminate. That put me right back in the closet." A year later he answered another ad, met someone he liked, but never heard back from him. Then an old high school friend came out to him, and bullied him out of his cave.

"I went to the bar in London, but after a while the mind games really started to depress me. When you say you're a farmer some of them turn right off; they think farmers are poor hicks. My assets are over a million dollars!" What exactly was he looking for? "A friend. What I'd envisioned was a lifetime friend, like my straight male friends when I was younger, only with the sexual part an added bonus. But for most of the people I met it was strictly a one-night thing."

After a while Lyle got up the nerve to put his own ad in *Farm & Country*, the first gay ad ever in the Ontario-wide paper. The message was in code: "30-ish male farmer seeks friendship with similar...." He threw away the replies that opened with sex-talk – "That's no way to start anything." Others were out of reach. A young farmer in eastern Ontario wrote that this was the first time he'd ever talked to anyone about being gay. They corresponded, and the other guy actually came by for a visit. "But his farm is there, mine is here. That's the way it goes."

What if Lyle actually did meet his long-awaited friend, and the man was free to come live here on the farm? "I don't know what I'd do. I know my parents wouldn't accept him. They don't talk about it any-more, but I'm sure they still hope I'll get married one of these days. I hate all this sneaking around; it makes me feel like a little kid."

Lyle has to go home now. Just before they close, the Chicago markets will often whip into a trading frenzy, and he doesn't want to be left out. Then he'll have to go out to the barn to do the evening chores. The hired man's supposed to do it, but – well, he's in his six-ties and doesn't much like the cold.

▶ 16 WE'LL BE WATCHING YOU

"SHORTLY AFTER WE ARRIVED HERE," SAYS JO, "A PHOTO-graph I was in – at a demonstration during the Oka siege – happened to get into the local paper. A couple of days later two guys came around in a truck. They appeared to be asking about some old grave-yard." Scarlet adds, "But it was pretty obvious they weren't paying any attention to the directions we gave them. Suddenly one of them asked was Jo the woman at the demonstration. She said she was. So where are you from, he asks, how long have you been here, and what's the status of your papers?" Jo: "It really shocked me, but I just laughed it off, I said everything's in order, there's no problem." Scarlet: "Then he said, 'Well, we'll be watching you,' and they took off."

Jo sits at the kitchen table, her hands folded before her. Scarlet leans back on her chair. It's a cool grey autumn day in Pictou County, Nova Scotia. The two of them met at university in England, where Jo taught social work, and Scarlet was studying for her Ph.D. in sociol-ogy. They moved in together on a small farm. Jo is English, Scarlet a Canadian who had temporary status in England. If they were to live together in either country, one of them would have to emigrate. Jo applied to Canadian immigration in London, as a social worker. Rejected. Then she applied as an independent farmer-entrepreneur, and got a six-month visa to buy a viable farm in Canada. Viability would be determined by her ability to get a mortgage. By now Scarlet had a teaching job in Halifax, and could co-sign for the loan. They found a farm; Jo applied for a mortgage. Rejected – the official implied that farm work might be a bit heavy for a woman.

With time running out, they came across a large former pig farm, but with an acre of raspberries – now *that* a woman could handle. The loan came through, and Jo was in. Now they've settled on another farm, 107 acres where they raise organic chickens, geese, pigs, goats, and cows. Most of the meat they sell direct to people in Halifax. Scarlet is forty-seven; Jo, now a Canadian citizen, is a year older.

"I always knew in some way that I wanted to be with women," says Jo, "but the self-hate was very strong. I kept thinking, oh no, I can't be one of *those*." Her first relationship at fifteen – "classically at boarding school" – nearly got her expelled; she survived only because she was so good at sports. But once she encountered the women's liberation movement, "I realized there were a great number of people around who were just like me. That was enormously liberating, on so many levels." And more than a little risky, it seemed. "I got sacked from two jobs because I was a lesbian, and I got picked up by the police a couple of times – it was no big deal, they were just harassing us." In a relationship at twenty-two, Jo had the other woman's father after her. "He took a couple of shots at me – with a *gun*." She laughs. "You can't imagine how rare that was in England."

From the prairies, Scarlet went to England with her husband, who'd been hired to teach at university there. Horrified at being invited to a tea for professors' wives, instead she went to a women's liberation meeting. Then she convinced her husband they must attend a meeting of the newborn Gay Liberation Front – in solidarity, of course. She left her husband shortly after, got involved with another man, a friend of theirs, and the first woman she slept with was his partner. This was the '70s; anything was possible.

Now that they're here to stay, how have they been accepted? "Well...." They look at each other. Scarlet replies, "I think people are reasonably tolerant as long as you don't do or say anything that provokes them." "You tend to be judged more by what you do as a farmer," Jo adds, "how well you care for your animals and that sort of thing." This morning they sent eighty of their chickens off to be slaughtered. Why don't they do it themselves? "We can't," says Jo. "Killing things is horrible." Scarlet adds, "Around here it's a measure of how serious you are as a farmer, whether or not you can kill animals. I guess we don't quite measure up in that respect." "But then we tend to be let off because we're women," Jo smiles. "Women have to be a little nurturing, don't they?"

The we'll-be-watching-you attitude that can be so unnerving also has its advantages. "There is an ethic here," says Jo, "that you have a duty to your neighbours. If we're having a bonfire, for example, people passing by on the road will slow down until they're clear on the source of the fire." Scarlet: "Or when we're unloading hay in the summer, if someone comes by they'll probably just get up on the wagon and help, you'll chat awhile then they'll be gone. Of course you're supposed to do the same in return." Jo: "When there's something going on at the local hall, all the women get called on to make sandwiches, cakes, and what not." She laughs. "Since there's two women in our household, we're supposed to do double!"

One of their continuing tasks is to confound traditional roles. Scarlet: "The one who has the money and fixes the machinery is always seen as the boss." Jo: "So we have to be careful about which one of us is being seen in which role. We listen to what people are saying, and once we realize someone's slotted one of us, we'll decide it's the other one's turn to be seen on the tractor."

Tonight they'll bring their chickens home, no longer chickens but chicken now, ready for the freezer. Scarlet says, a little ruefully, "I suppose the best we can hope for is that while they were with us, they had a decent life."

▶ 17 **THAT LITTLE COMFORT**

THE RAIN STOPS; THE AIR IS COOL AND SWEET. TREES, house, and barn are silhouettes, with light fading from the summer sky. A grey sandhill crane floats overhead, in slow motion. We're in

Sandra's market garden, about an hour's drive south of Winnipeg, Manitoba.

Hobbling between the rows – this morning she sprained her ankle in an old post hole – Sandra points out examples of nature's elegant logic at work. "One of the things you can do in a small space like this is to plant a fast-growing cool weather plant like radish or lettuce almost on top of a plant that grows much slower, like the tomato. By the time your tomato plant spreads its leaves, you've already harvested your lettuce."

The garden wraps round an old barn. Under the sagging eaves, drums catch the rain – it's plentiful these days, but drought is always a threat here. The vegetable garden occupies less than an acre of land, but this summer it will feed over a hundred people from tightly spaced rows of organically grown lettuce, beans, eggplant, broccoli, tomatoes, celery, carrots, potatoes, squash, parsley and other herbs.

Currently popping up all over Canada, community-shared agri-culture projects (CSAs) are meant to spread the financial risks of food-production among consumers as well as growers, to bypass profit-hungry distributors, and to provide consumers with fresh, locally grown and usually organic food. Members buy a share in the output of the garden, giving the grower some much-needed cash up front, and in return they receive a portion of the garden's varied yield over the growing season.

The climate here can be cruelly capricious. Everything is done by hand, from late winter to fall, including deliveries – each week Sandra hauls a bag of freshly harvested produce to each member in the city. Last year she did it alone, but this summer with the CSA tripling in size she hired an assistant. "Trouble is, I insist on paying her the same as me, so it's broken the bank. I can't have her in for the next couple of weeks. I'll just have to wait and see how the market goes." She's taken a table at Winnipeg's first all-organic farmers' mar-ket. "I also make wild fruit preserves and herb vinegars." She laughs. "It gives me something to do in my spare time."

I ask about her journey as a sexual being. "Well," she says, "my first *voluntary* sexual experience was with a girl, when I was about seven. I sometimes wonder if I would have been doing that so early if I hadn't already been sexually abused by then. But I had no concept at all of being a lesbian. I assumed I'd go through life as a heterosexual, get married, and have children. I got pregnant at fifteen, and for the next eight years or so I had male lovers. It's strange, my friends were all lesbians, they were the only people I was really interested in – but I just couldn't take that one more step to being sexual with a woman. Then I fell in love with a woman, and after that everything seemed so simple."

Sandra shares her life, and the land here, with her partner, Cathy, and several other lesbians who own the land jointly.* Cathy works full-time as a carpenter in Winnipeg. Each of the land-holders has her own house, some distance from the others and complete with a lavender outhouse. This spring Sandra created a stir by acquiring the first flush toilet in the group. "I'm forty-eight, and I'm doing this work that's so demanding physically I can hardly believe it, so it's really nice to have that little comfort."

How comfortable is she out here, does she feel she belongs? "It can go either way. For instance, a young woman who wanted to work in the garden got lost on the way here and ended up at the dairy farm next door. 'Oh,' said the woman there, 'You must be looking for that *lesbian colony*' – apparently her tone was really nasty, she made it sound like a cult or something. This woman never waves – they're church people."

On the other hand? "The woman who works with me on the garden is also from around here. When I hired her fourteen-year-old daughter to cut our grass, she asked her mom if Cathy and I were related. 'Well,' said the mom, 'Actually they're a couple.' I asked her how her daughter took that, and she said it was no big deal, 'you're not the first lesbians she's known.' I'm pretty sure that's the first time she'd ever acknowledged us that directly. I thought it was kind of nice." She chuckles. "As long as we don't try to volunteer for the fire department I think we'll be okay."

---

* More on them in Ch 30

What sustains her here? "I love gardening. I hope I can do it in a way that won't work me to death. I don't know. Will people pay what the food really costs to produce? Sure, you can get a lettuce from California for fifty cents, but if you look at the real costs – to the earth, to low-paid migrant workers, even to the long-term health of consumers here – the costs are enormous. Only if people start to understand that can I keep on doing this work that I really love. We'll see."

It's nearly dark now. In silence we watch tiny pulses of light glow and die over the swaying grass – a wondrous dance of fireflies. The wind is rising. Another storm is due.

18 A LITTLE GAY WORLD

HEAPS OF CLOUD SPRAWL ACROSS A PANAVISION SKY, their shadows skating over smooth grey-green bumps and creases. I'm in the Cypress Hills, in the southwest corner of Saskatchewan. Two of Jim's glossy auburn horses mosey over, snuffle at me, then resume grazing near the rusting hulk of a prairie dinosaur, some huge abandoned farm machine. The warm air is laden with sweet sage.

Down below, a slow creek winds among the wolf willows, past the Spring Valley Guest Ranch. In the kitchen Jim Saville presides over dinner preparations in cowboy boots, creased jeans with a big shiny country-and-western belt buckle, and a long apron. Sixteen birdwatchers are expected for dinner tonight, plus the ten guests who are booked in at the ranch.

Jim is forty-one. He was born about a mile from here, where his parents and brother still ranch. He went to school in Eastend, population 700. "That was a miserable time," he says. "I never fit. What I most wanted was to be a dancer, but of course I didn't dare tell anyone. When I started to catch on that I was attracted to men, I used to cry myself to sleep at night. I didn't understand how I could have these feelings that were supposed to be so terrible."

At nineteen Jim went off to university in Saskatoon, and there he made his first gay connection. "I was so petrified, I put the whole thing on hold again until I was twenty-six. It's sad to think of so many years lost like that." Finally he found a gay support group, and "I've never looked back." When he came out to his mother, she said, "God burdens the ones he loves the most," her brand of acceptance. He waited a year to tell his father, whom he saw as "kind of a redneck cowboy." By this time Jim had a lover in Saskatoon, where he lived. "When I told my father I was gay, all he said was, 'What's your room-mate going to think?'"

After university, various jobs and travels, Jim set about realizing his dream, to open a bed and breakfast. Six years ago he found a suitable house for sale, and had it hauled on a flatbed truck to a piece of land he owned in the hills near his childhood home.

His 1,000 acres nestle in the valley and rise up onto the plateau, "the bench." He feeds over 5,000 people a year in his restaurant, many of them from the region. "I produce as much of the food as I can here; you don't just pop into town for a loaf of bread." (It's twenty-five miles' drive to Maple Creek, where Jim also teaches line-dancing at a local straight bar.) Bread is home-made, vegetables are grown in a big garden beside the house, eggs are gathered from the chicken coop, and the lambs and geese I watch playing out there in the grass will soon be on the menu.

When he left Saskatoon, Jim kept in touch with friends. "But it's a long way. My city friends can't fathom what I'm doing out here in the hills, and they don't seem all that interested in finding out." There are no gay people nearby? "Either they get out as soon as they can," says Jim, "or they just hang on, living at home with their parents. It's sad. I'd like to help them somehow, but any kind of contact would scare the life out of them." Now and then he gets an obscene phone call. "I don't pay any attention. If you dwell too much on these things, you can go crazy. If I had a partner with me here, I know there'd be a whole new set of problems with visibility." His closest friends in the area are straight women.

Jim estimates that about forty percent of his guests are gay or lesbian, and the proportion is rising. But there's one spectacular long weekend each year in August when the place is all ours. The annual event draws gay men and lesbians from as far away as Vancouver and Winnipeg; last year over sixty showed up, and this year Jim expects more. They overflow the guest house, the cabins, and the tipis out back, spilling into the meadows with their tents. There are games, picnics, hayrides, concerts, and dancing in the big barn. To feed this multitude, Jim's parents and straight friends pitch in – his mum in the kitchen, his dad helps out with the horses, the friends cook and dish up food.

"For that one weekend," says Jim, "it's a little gay world out here. It's a chance to be totally relaxed, out in the sun and the fresh air, doing things we can't do anywhere else, not even in the city. Like a high-heel race – can you imagine trying to get away with something like that in a city park?"

The birdwatchers have just arrived, sixteen of them, hungry after a full day trekking in the hills. The lesbian staffperson got time off to attend a twelve-step picnic. That leaves her coworker, a young gay man from the city, to throw on a clean shirt and wait tables, which he does with suitable attitude. In the kitchen, Jim prepares salads.

About that high-heel race. In these ancient, isolated hills, how can there be enough shoes? "Oh well," says Jim, "I just go into the second-hand clothing store in Maple Creek and buy up all the high-heels they've got." He chuckles. "They're really hard to come by in the bigger sizes."

▶ 19 LES P'TITS GARS

"WE HAD THIS GAY COUPLE, ONE OF THEM WAS QUITE flamboyant, a real queen. And we had this other couple, very straight, the man was a minister. When they all sat down to breakfast I held my breath. But by the time it was over, they were exchanging addresses. At that point we decided to stop worrying. Our attitude now is, if you don't like it, the door is there."

In the Laurentian mountains north of Montréal, l'Auvent Bleu sits at the intersection of a small river and two roads. Oui's and Non's sprout everywhere, signs of the sovereignty referendum campaign now in full steam. It's late September; the valleys and hills are splashed with red, gold, and purple. After an unusually dry summer the river at the bottom of the garden is low, but still passable by canoe. Frost has already touched the garden. In the greenhouse fat crimson tomatoes still ripen on the vine.

Your Bed and Breakfast hosts are Jean-François Boissoneault and Luc Martin, with three guest rooms. Round here the two of them are known as "les p'tits gars de l'Auvent Bleu." Les p'tits gars translates as "the boys," l'auvent bleu as "the blue awning." Since the boys took over the place, they've taken down all the blue awnings to let in more sun. It floods the dining room, at breakfast prepared by Luc – granola and yogurt, fresh-baked carrot muffins. He's a vegetarian, or what a friend calls a lacto-ovo-homo. Jean-François has already left for work.

Luc is thirty-six. He was born to a Catholic family in Willowbunch, a tiny francophone town in south Saskatchewan. "I always felt like an odd duck, and I used to think it was because I was the only one in my family not interested in farming." Nor was he interested in girls, though he had "the obligatory girlfriend" in high school. Then he went off to university in New Brunswick, the only place where he could take a common law degree in French. "I also wanted to go someplace where no one knew me, so it would be easier to be myself." At twenty-one Luc had his first sexual experience. To his surprise, most of his friends in Moncton also turned out to be gay. A couple of years later, with law degree in hand, he got a job with the federal court challenges program in Ottawa. "The city was just the right size for me. I had a good job, and for the first time in my life I had money in my pocket. I loved it there."

Jean-François is thirty-two. He grew up in Rouyn-Noranda. The youngest of eight kids, he was having sex-play with both boys and girls from the start of his teens. "I didn't think of it as gay or straight; it was just the way it was." When he was fourteen the family moved south to Hull, across the river from Ottawa. At nineteen he left home to live with a woman. "I really loved her, but I also told her I was attracted to men. She was quite accepting of that." In due course the household included his male lover.

One night eleven years ago, Jean-François dropped in to a gay bar in Ottawa. He and Luc exchanged smiles, and talked. Jean-François suggested they go for a coffee. Can't, said Luc, I'm waiting for a friend. You've been waiting a long time, said Jean-François, come on. Sorry, said Luc, I promised him I'd be here. "That's when he got my heart," says Jean-François, "Honesty like that, you don't find it every day." In the course of conversation he touched Luc on the chest. Luc: "I never felt anything like that before; my knees actually went weak. What a cliché!" Luc wrote his number on a matchbook. "Of course I thought that's the last I'll ever see of him." Jean-François called the next morning, early. "Luc was the turning point for me, the first time I knew what I really wanted." Three years later they bought a condominium together in Hull.

Jean-François: "I asked my brother – he's in real estate – to find us a cottage in the Laurentians, just for weekends. One day he called; he said, there's this place you have to see. It wasn't a cottage, it was a big house, a Bed and Breakfast with five bedrooms and eighty-seven acres, completely out of the question. But we decided to go anyway, just for laughs. As soon as I saw it I wanted to live here the rest of my life. I do that, I go on impulse, but not Luc. I was afraid to ask him what he thought." They drove halfway home in silence. Then Luc said, "I want it." Within five days they'd bought l'Auvent Bleu. A week later Luc panicked. "I grew up in a small town, and I swore I'd never live in a place like that again. There wasn't even a village here, nothing but an intersection!" Within a month they'd rented out the condo and moved. Luc: "I know now never to say never, but I can't imagine ever wanting to live in the city again."

For the first couple of years they built their B&B business, renovating the house, getting the septic system fixed, adding a deck by the pool, working on the garden, publicizing l'Auvent Bleu in gay and mainstream publications. To make ends meet, Luc continued to work part-time on the court challenges program, doing as many of his assignments as he could at home. Jean-François worked a year as a flight attendant, flying out of Mirabel international airport in the south Laurentians. "That was a rough year; Luc was gone half the time, I was gone the other half; we hardly ever saw each other." Then the Tories killed the court challenges program. Their mortgage still loomed, and their car died.

Jean-François got a job at the big Mont Tremblant lodge, about an hour's drive by twisting valley roads. It's currently expanding into a major international resort and conference centre, with a staff of 1,500 that now includes Luc on the front desk. "The fact that we're a couple has to be the worst kept secret around there." Jean-François: "When they interviewed me for the job to manage the front desk, they asked me if it might be a problem for me to discipline my spouse [conjoint]. I was quite shocked that they would ask me that, but then I was happy that our relationship was out in the air, so I wouldn't have to face it later on. I said it was unlikely Luc would ever have to be disciplined, but in any case it wouldn't be a problem." Luc: "It depends what they mean by discipline – it could be fun." They laugh.

The two of them are good friends with Jean-François' ex, her husband, and their three kids. The husband kisses them both when they visit. Luc: "We've told him he's wasted on heterosexuality." Most of their friends live in Ottawa-Hull, but recently they've become close with two lesbians, Diane and Maud, with a farm Bed and Breakfast half an hour from here.* Luc's oldest and closest friend lives a couple of thousand miles away, in Saskatchewan.†

Luc calls Jean-François' mother his second mother. "One time when she was here, and Jean-François was leaving for work, she said to Luc, 'Go on, give him a kiss like you would if I wasn't here.'" The only one of Luc's family nearby, his brother, visits often with the kids. "We have mixed parties, gay and straight, so the kids see how varied people can be – she's with her, he's with him, she's with him – it's all quite normal to them."

---

* More on them in Ch 28
† More on him in Ch 18

If they could afford it, Luc and Jean-François would both quit their jobs in a moment. Luc: "When you're on the front line at a big hotel, people think they can yell at you, turn their back on you; they throw a shit fit over the smallest thing. We'll take our B&B people any day; they're much more respectful when they're in your place." But business at L'Auvent Bleu is quiet through the winter. It's a little too far from the ski hills, and to host even small workshops they'd need a few more rooms. To get free of their outside jobs, either they'll have to invest heavily in this place – build cabins, enlarge the dining room and kitchen to accommodate a restaurant – or buy a bigger place. Either way, it will put them deeper in debt.

Luc: "But look, coming out is a risk. Same when you make your life with someone. And moving out here, with no experience in B&B. Now it's the same thing again. If we could see the future, life wouldn't be so interesting, would it?"

▶ 20 THE FRONT LINE

"THIS KID CAME UP TO ME IN THE CLASSROOM, HE SAID, 'Sticking your dick up someone's ass is real sick, isn't it.' I said, 'Get out, don't come back here today.' He knew that kind of talk isn't allowed in my classroom, and it wasn't the first time he'd said things like that. He went to the office, and the principal called me out from the classroom; he wanted to know why the kid was sent out. I told him what he'd said. The principal said, 'Yeah? So what's your problem?' Would you believe it?

"To cool off I went to the staff room. One of the teachers happened to be talking about Tommy [Sexton – a member of the popular satirical troupe Codco, who'd just died of AIDS, having asked that his ashes be dropped from a plane]. He was saying, 'Fucking faggot couldn't be buried like everyone else, he had to spread his fucking virus all over Newfoundland.' I just lost it, I said, 'I've had enough of you, you're supposed to be an educator but for God's sake, you're no better than Hitler!' I went on and on, to the point where another teacher took my arm and tried to get me out of there. Do you think I could teach that day?"

"Janet" and her partner "Ellen," also a teacher in St John's, are on the front line in a bitter struggle for the hearts and minds of the young. Being the capital of Newfoundland and a sophisticated city, St John's hardly qualifies as rural or small town. But a number of Newfoundlanders assured me that the province is still dominated not only by the church but also by conservative rural values. In any case, the account of how Janet and Ellen came to be on the front line, and of the day-to-day challenges they face there, stands for many stories I heard from rural gay and lesbian teachers across Canada.

Janet is thirty-eight. She grew up in a village of about thirty families on the west coast of Newfoundland. "I always knew I was different," she says. "I was strongly attracted to my kindergarten teacher, and from six years old to about ten I insisted on being called Tommy – I refused to answer to Janet." Under pressure, she started dating boys. "But I also pursued the woman next door. I had such a crush on her I just kept after her until we had an affair. She was twenty-five; I was twelve. Since it was always me pursuing her, never for one minute did I feel abused. But I made the mistake of asking a teacher what it meant to be gay. He said, 'Oh my God, they're sick, they're perverted, they're child molesters!' So I started to think I must be sick, and within a few months I really was. It was about that time I found out I was adopted, and all I could think was I can't bear this, I've got to get out. I went into the woods and cut myself, really badly, my arms, my face. I ended up in the psychiatric unit at the children's hospital in St John's." Eight months later she returned home, strong enough to survive but no clearer on her sexuality.

Over the next two decades Janet dated men, secretly sent away for any material she could get on homosexuality, played on a women's baseball team, slept on the sly with a girlfriend who, like her, also had a boyfriend, and drank. In her late teens she decided to track down her biological mother. Through an accidental remark, she learned that the woman she was looking for was actually a fellow ball-player – a married woman and a closet lesbian. "There were lots of them in

Cornerbrook, all of them either married or dating men, but then they'd go off on their skidoos and sleep with each other." In fact Janet had felt drawn to this particular woman. "My God," she says, "I could've slept with my own mother!"

St John's had come to represent a safe harbour to her, so she moved there. "I love being near the ocean. It's not the same on the west coast, where you're always aware of land on the other side. This is really the *ocean*, it's like being on the edge of the world. So I'd take my bottle of rum, and I'd go sit out on Flat Rock. I'd be absolutely drenched from the spray – the power of it, my God – and I'd dare the sea to take me."

Six years ago she dried out at a treatment centre in Toronto. By then she was teaching. A year later she met Ellen at a Take Back the Night march, and within another year they'd exchanged rings and bought a house on a steep street in St John's, where they live with their dog Rosie. The house is painted in brilliant we're-here-dammit shades of blue and yellow. "The only people who like it are my brother and gay men," says Janet.

On a drizzly Sunday morning, bells call the faithful to mass down the hill. Thirty-seven, Ellen was born here in St John's. All of her immediate family still live close by. "As a child I was very much what you'd call a tomboy. I had slingshots and a pocket knife, and all my friends were boys. But then as soon as it started to dawn on me that I was queer, I set about unqueering myself. I'd sit in front of the mirror every morning and curl my hair; I had incredibly long red nails and very high heels – and in my late twenties I had a lot of casual sex with men, *a lot*. I really did a good job of hiding. I tell you, *no one* ever suspected me."

She got a job as secretary in a school, studied for her teacher's certificate in her spare time, and now teaches at the same school, as well as working toward a master's degree in women's studies at the university. She's out now to family and friends, and works with the Newfoundland Amazon Network to get a lesbian resource centre going. But as a teacher she's still in hiding. The province has no legislated human rights protection for gay and lesbian people, and rigidly conservative churches still maintain a stranglehold on the schools here. Recently the government announced its intentions to break this hold. For Ellen it can't happen soon enough.

"If I stood up in family life class and said I'm a lesbian – even if I talked positively about homosexuality – I'd be in awful deep trouble. I've overheard teachers saying things about us to students that, if they were talking about a black person or a particular religion, people would see it as supporting hate. But when we're the target it's perfectly acceptable! And there I am, keeping my mouth shut. There are kids in the class, I'm sure they're homosexual or lesbian, but by denying who I am, I'm doing even less to support them than a decent straight teacher might do. I feel bad about that, really bad."

For similar reasons, Janet hasn't come out at school either. But because she won't keep silent in the face of bigotry, "Three severely homophobic male teachers decided to get me. It was almost as if they'd planned it, hardly a day would pass without some ugly joke about women or gays from one of these men." When the best she could get from the principal was "Oh, lighten up," Janet transferred to another school. And ran into the same problem. "It puts me in such a rage, I can't be much use as a teacher. If I'm to stick it out, I really need a little help." She's asked her teachers' union to organize province-wide workshops on homophobia in the schools. It would be a start.

"I don't know what I'd do," says Janet, "if I couldn't get to the ocean." Flat Rock slides away, glistening black, into the Atlantic. An indolent swell rises and falls – ten feet perhaps? – slow, hypnotic, like breathing. This is a calm day, unusually warm and clear for mid-October.

We're standing well back from the height of the swell. Janet indicates a spot below, licked by cold spray. That's where she used to sit with her rum, daring the sea to take her. It could have. It does, indifferently, without discrimination. Despite all the warnings, people go too close, the ocean reaches out, they're gone. And the next land is Europe.

June

JUNE GETS COWS PREGNANT. "SOME OF THE MEN THINK it's a weird thing for a woman to be doing, but they don't give me a hard time about it, not so much any more." She's an artificial insemination technician in Pictou County, Nova Scotia.

She and her partner, Judy, grew up in a coal town that was gradually being eaten away by the strip mine. Both dropped out of school, and became friends in their teens. June had no doubt she was a lesbian. Says Judy, "I guess I was trying to be asexual. To look at me, the way I dressed, you could hardly tell what sex I was. And I didn't care a whole lot either." After they'd lived together two years, June threatened that if Judy didn't "come across," she'd go out and find herself a man. They both laugh. They've been together twenty-one years. June is forty-one; Judy, forty-four.

Moving to a small town on the Northumberland Straits, they built their own loghouse on twenty acres of wooded land. "We had no money and no electricity," recalls Judy. "All we had was a chainsaw, a handsaw, and a hammer. But I guess it worked out okay." Their house is warm, solid, and comfortable. They share it with three small dogs.

"When we moved here," says June, "everyone said, you're crazy, you'll never get a job." From two days after their arrival they've never been without. Judy was turned down for a few – "Could be 'cause I'm a lesbian, but it's pretty hard to pin down that kind of thing." She's worked the past six years at a local group home, until a month ago when the owners sold it, and she was refused a small raise. Now she hopes to make a career of her passion – writing, singing, and playing her own music. "Used to be protest songs, but now I'm content if I can just make people feel good. People can use a little of that these days." She plays guitar, fiddle, and piano, and she's learning to read music. "Up to now I've just memorized my tunes, but now I'll be able to actually write them down."

That leaves June, the AI tech, as the steady earner in the household. She works for a breeders' co-op, with her own zone to service.

She does her rounds of the dairy farms by truck, with a freezer full of sperm collected from the breeders' prize bulls. AI is cheaper, safer, and genetically more effective for farmers than housing and maintaining their own bulls.

One of the standard arguments against homosexuality is that it's unnatural. In her work, June regularly encounters evidence to the contrary. To get the best draw of semen from a bull, the goal is to achieve the best ejaculation possible. It happens that some bulls would rather mount a steer or another bull than any available cow; they choose a male every time – and the breeders, some of them rabidly anti-gay, never make a peep of protest.

Wayne

"FROM THE TIME I WAS TWELVE I KNEW I WAS GAY, NO question about it. But I also grew up in a good Catholic home in Newfoundland, and I learned how to play the game. I joined the Mounted Police, I married, I had two wonderful kids. When I finally began to realize how much damage I'd done to myself, how many walls I'd built, that's when I started to come out – nine years ago." Two years later he met his partner. Wayne is forty-two; Lloyd, thirty-one.

Five years ago they moved from the east coast to Yellowknife, a promotional transfer for Wayne with the RCMP. Lloyd works at a local hotel. Given the Mounties' record, which includes extensive surveillance and harassment of gay people, how has Wayne managed? "For a long time that was part of playing the game, and like I said, I did it well. I guess I must have been one of your more 'sensitive' Mounties. When I came out to some of the men I used to work with, they'd say, 'Well now, that makes sense, you always did bake the best bread!'" He laughs. "But you know, some of them actually apologized for anything they'd said in the past that might have offended or hurt me – I was really touched by that."

I pursue the awkward matter of the anti-gay witch hunts, more than two decades of them. "Yes, we were a repressive organization. I'd like to think we didn't know better, and it's not something the Mounted Police are proud of," says Wayne. "But this is now – we gay men and women are here, we're proud, and we're staying. Just watch me; I can do the job better than anyone else. And I'm here to tell you, a thing like that won't happen again."

Yellowknife is an odd hybrid of capital city and frontier town. Says Lloyd, "We were pretty sure coming up here would either cement our relationship or break it." Wayne adds, "We have to depend on each other a lot more than we would in a bigger place, that's for sure. Sometimes it's not easy." Lloyd: "One night we were set to go to a movie, but somebody warned us: you can't do that, it's Valentine's Day! And they were right – the only people who can be out together that night as couples are straight!" Wayne: "I wouldn't think of reaching over the table in a restaurant here and taking Lloyd's hand. You'd be in big trouble. There's so much work to be done."

This is not how I imagined a Mountie, not at all. "We have to educate people," he says. "They have to learn that being gay is not a choice. There's still so little positive material available in the schools and public libraries. The young need access to good gay literature; they shouldn't have to lose all those years like I did."

Wayne has few illusions. "We've certainly gained some ground in terms of acceptance. But the battle lines are drawn, they really are. The fundamentalist right is just beginning to show how much damage it can do. I'm afraid it's our brothers and sisters in the small communities who'll suffer most from the bigotry. But for my part I will not go back into that closet – no matter what. No way. Never again."

Jerry

A TEEN-AGE CLIENT HAS ASKED JERRY'S YOUNG ASSIS-tant to do her hair like what's-her-name on *Beverley Hills 90210* – she's brought a photo. Jerry tells the assistant, "Go ahead, you can do it." She does the cut; the client is ecstatic and so is Jerry. "God, if this *90210* thing catches on, maybe we'll get a lineup in here."

From the 1700s on, Minto in central New Brunswick has lived and died by its coal mines. A few years ago the opening of a huge new strip mine lifted spirits for a moment, but the coal is extracted by giant machines, and few people are required. "If I'd been straight," he says,

"I would've got married and worked in the mines. So there you go." Jerry packed up and left, several times, but each time he's come back, most recently with his partner, Bruce. "I always got homesick for my family," he says. His mother drops by to lend him her old Cadillac so he can show us around. We stop by his sister's pizza place to pick up supper. Another sister and a sister-in-law work there too. While we wait for our combo plates, one of his brothers drops by with his son, and the chat flies every which way. This is why Jerry came home.

He's thirty-seven; Bruce is fifty. They met at Sunset Beach in Vancouver, but disagree on exactly who picked up whom. Gradually moving west from Ontario, Bruce had done well in trucking, then made a couple of good deals in real estate. Jerry grew up here, one of nine kids, his coal miner dad making fifty dollars a week. "That's where my survival instinct comes from, growing up poor. You do what you have to to stay afloat." Jerry smokes a lot, talks fast, there's an urgency about him. "I was very feminine as a kid, I practically grew up in a dress – my older sisters used to get a big kick out of dressing me up." When he was eighteen his mother's sister helped him come out, in Montreal. "She was a go-go dancer, an amazing woman. She took me to all the clubs and showed me the gay world up there." He's still ambivalent about city life. "Here everyone knows your business. In the city no one cares, so take your pick."

When they moved back east, Bruce bought their house here with the adjoining beauty salon, and the camp near the lake. He also loaned Jerry the money to start up his business. He seems a little lost here, doesn't quite know what to do with himself. But not Jerry – "I can't sit still for long, I have to move forward. I really want the business to grow." His urgency is partly driven by health. Twelve years ago, Jerry tested positive for HIV.

"I was out to all my family by then, but when I told them about the HIV they were devastated; they thought I must be dying. I guess I must come from good stock. I take fewer chemicals than I used to, but other than that I haven't changed much. I just live, day to day." In a small town like this, word must get around. "At first I was afraid no one would come into the shop, I even thought maybe I'd have to run.

But – here I am." No jokes, no questions? "Oh, there's all kinds of that. I just deal with it head on. I'm the only gay man most of them have ever talked to. They want to know things like, which of you is the man? That's fine by me, if it's how they get to be comfortable with me."

In another two weeks it'll be Hallowe'en. Bruce will dress up as an old crone, in a fully concealing head mask. Jerry will shave his ample moustache and transform himself into Rachel, an elegant middle-aged person with a hairpiece as thick as a horse's tail that cascades from her meticulously coiffed head. When they're ready, they'll walk a few blocks up the street to the Legion, for a drink and a dance.

▶ ## 22 ODD JOBS TOO

Robert

"EVERY DAY I'D COME TO WORK IN A NEW SILK JUMPSUIT. I'd get into my cage, I'd take the men down into the mine, and every day the same thing, I'd end up with the clothes pulled off me. I'd go back up totally nude except for my workboots. Next day I'd come to work in a new outfit. Every day it was the same thing." In a northern mining town, how did he come to have so many silk jumpsuits? "Oh," says Robert, "that's from when I was a stripper in Toronto."

Robert is a miner near Timmins, in northeast Ontario. "We do it in the hole," he says, feigning surprise at the laugh that erupts from the gay and lesbian friends gathered here in a basement rec room. To them he's Bobby. He's francophone, but quite at ease in English. As far back as he can remember he was attracted to men, had his first sex at twelve, and his first lover at eighteen. "I told my mom; we had a big fight; I left home and went to Toronto. Leo* and me, we were strippers there." This was in the early '70s. After a few years Robert came home to Timmins, broke up with his lover and, under intense pressure from his mother, married. "My wife knew. We were married

---

* More on him in Ch 36

three years, we had two kids, then I went out to find myself a man."

"André" picked him up on the highway, hitchhiking. He's also a miner. They dated; Robert moved in and got a divorce. His daughter lived with them for five years, his son for sixteen. "I had to tone down my lifestyle a bit for them, I even told my gay friends not to come over for a while. Now André will tell my son, no, you can't have the car, and then I'll tell him, oh sure, go ahead. But he still doesn't want his friends to know; he's afraid they'll tease him." Robert's father, who works at the same mine, disowned him. Eventually he came around, but still had concerns like, "What's the correct way for me to behave with your man?" and "He doesn't beat you, does he?"

Out of his cage now, Robert runs an underground level at the mine. From engineer's blueprints, he directs a crew in opening and blasting new tunnels to the gold and copper ore. A few weeks ago, the roof fell in and an enormous boulder pinned him to the ground. He was alone. "I couldn't feel anything in my leg. I pushed the rock off me – God knows how – climbed over the front-end loader, walked maybe half a mile and phoned for help. That was the closest I've come to getting it in twenty-four years. But you have to go back in, that's the job."

Every year in May, on the Queen's Birthday, Bobby throws a drag party at their summer cottage. It draws men from as far away as Toronto, with enough baggage for an ocean cruise. Weeks of work go into costumes and lip-synch routines. Statuesque (if a little bulky) as Whitney Huston, Robert did "I Will Always Love You."

Robert's daughter asked him if she could attend the famous event. "'Are you *crazy?*' I said. I wouldn't let her near the place. So the party's underway, and who shows up but some of her friends – someone else invited them. They had a ball;, then they went home and told her about it. She wouldn't talk to me for a week. Kids. What can you do, eh?"

"Lee"

"LEE" RAISES HOGS IN SOUTH SASKATCHEWAN, A farrow-to-finish operation – after this they're pork. She grew up farming in Ontario. "As a kid I always wished I could be a boy. I could see they had so much more freedom; they could do whatever they wanted. And I always preferred men's clothes – they're better made and better cut." At the moment she's wearing black jeans and a roomy white shirt. We're sitting on the porch of the cottage that she and her partner rent, by a lake in the Qu'Appelle valley. It's evening, mid-June. Waves lap at the shore, a soothing background. Lee's motorcycle is parked in the drive.

"When I was young my father included me in all the farm work, he taught me how to fix the tractor and all that. But as soon as puberty hit I was sent into the house to learn girl's work. I really hated that." This was a pentecostal household. Roles and rules were absolute, and Lee knew enough to keep her dreams and desires to herself. "Since I wanted nothing to do with marriage, I just figured I had no choice but to stay single the rest of my life." An outsider at school, she never dated, but immersed herself in church, the only community she knew. She prayed constantly to be saved.

Lee went away to university, got a degree in agriculture, came west to Saskatoon, got a masters degree in plant genetics, and met her partner, "Gail." Gail didn't know she was native until she was twenty-one, her mother having lost her status by marrying a European. When federal law changed to allow the reclaiming of status, Gail chose not to. "It doesn't mean anything to me. I'm what they call an apple – red on the outside, white on the inside. I can make bannock, but that's about it."

Nor did she define herself as a young lesbian. "When a girl-friend told me she was attracted to me, I warned her if she came near me I'd beat the shit out of her." By fourteen she'd been sexually abused, she quit school, and she was an alcoholic. "I was a mess. I felt I had to choose – either end my life or do something with it." At six-teen she entered Baptist bible college. "I was desperate for love, and some kind of structure. The church provided both – they adopted me really; they were very supportive." At university, and troubled about her sexuality, Gail called the student help line. Lee answered. They became friends, and then lovers. Gail: "She came from a pentecostal background too, so we had a common language. That made her safe to me." Lee is thirty-one; Gail, thirty-seven.

Lee manages the hog barn for its owners, raising hogs from birth to market. The job includes wrestling 250-pound pigs onto the scales, feeding, cleaning, health care, welding broken pens, electrical work, and carpentry. "But my father would still dismiss anything I have to say about farming; he still maintains it's man's work. I really have to stop trying to please him; it just doesn't work."

A few months ago she came out to her parents, by letter. They fired back a nasty response that included a reference to her having ended up in the dirt with the pigs. Since then, silence. As always, she is sharply reminded to keep her reality to herself. "Trouble is," she says, "what you conceal, you also deny. If it's your relationship you're denying, that can do a whole lot of damage. When Gail and I are out in public together, we're both conscious of keeping each other at arm's length. One time I got too close and she actually pushed me away. It takes a while to recover from that when you get home."

Where do they stand with their God now, and the church? Gail: "I'm still not sure whether it's a sin to be gay. We're all created in sin, and we're all going to sin – homosexuals no more and no less than heterosexuals. But I won't end this relationship; it means too much to me. When the time comes, I'll just have to be responsible for it before God."

Lee: "I still like the idea of the church as a family. But as long they can only see me as a sin and not as a person, I just don't feel welcome there. And I'm less and less willing to risk their rejection. It's hard to hide who I am when I show up at church in a suit and tie – some people even call me 'sir'!"

The two of them will be heading for the city soon, both of them to go back to school. Lee has mixed feelings about the move. "I'd really like to be more out, and you can do that in the city; it's so much more anonymous there. On the other hand, what if you're in trouble and people just turn their backs? Here there's always someone around to lend a hand – even if they don't approve of you. I like being connected; I like knowing my neighbours; it's what I remember as a kid. I'd be really sorry to lose that."

Gerry

"WHEN YOU'RE LIVING OUT IN A LOGGING CAMP FOR months with these guys, it can be tough. Some of them are gorgeous, and they'll parade around nude after a shower. There's been a few even came on to me when they were drunk. But I'd never touch them, no way. Can you imagine what might happen when they sobered up?"

Gerry works in the woods back of the Okanagan Valley, in central British Columbia. He's forty-six. He and a few friends are gathered at the home of a gay couple, high above Vernon. The long lake far below turns gold in the waning light. Gerry's just back from a rodeo; he has a thing for cowboys. He rolls his eyes and sighs, "It was *wonderful.*"

He grew up in the Okanagan, logging and farming from his teens. And he knew he had feelings for men. "My family, everyone I knew was evangelical Christian. I believed in God, and I was taught that in his eyes homosexuality was a terrible sin; it was as bad as murder." But his feelings had their own imperative, so he had lovers in secret. "The way I felt about myself – so dirty and ashamed – my relationships didn't stand a chance." He decided to share his secret with a relative he thought he could trust. "They wouldn't even let me into their home anymore. They said they had to protect their children." And as good Christians, they informed on him to his parents. "The shame and guilt were – [he shakes his head] – well, I became suicidal."

At twenty-two Gerry escaped. For the first time in his life he met another human being, a woman friend, who told him it was okay to be gay. Even so, at thirty-six he married, and had a son. "I still wanted so much to please my family; I still wanted to change and please God." The marriage lasted two years. "It's only in the last few years that I've really begun to heal, with lots of help from counsellors and friends. I had to redefine the way I saw God, not as cruel and judgemental, but as a gentle, loving God who made me who I am." Another survivor of religious abuse, back from hell.

As a logger Gerry has felled and bucked trees – disentangled them from the brush and stripped off their branches – he's worked as a safety inspector, and now he runs a grapple skidder, a brute of a tractor that drags logs clear of the woods. Is this not a dangerous place to be gay? "Surprisingly not. The thing is, I'd already worked with these guys for years, we'd gone fishing together, we'd been out, had a few beers – they already knew me. When they found out I was gay, they just seemed to accept it. Some of them will even ask me who I'm dating, and how it's going. One time I overheard a new man telling my boss there was no way he'd work with a faggot. My boss told him if he ever gave me a hard time, he'd have to deal with him as well. It's that kind of thing makes you feel it's worthwhile to be out."

Logging is a major employer in British Columbia, and an extremely hot issue. I've just come from the Pacific side of Vancouver Island, where the struggle to preserve the last remaining old-growth forests in Clayoquot Sound has escalated to the international arena. A little nervously, I ask Gerry where this particular logger stands.

"I actually went out there," he replies, "to see for myself what all the fighting was about. Of course it shouldn't be cut. It doesn't have to be cut. The guys I know would never log a place like that. But it's not us making the decisions; it's somebody off in a board room, or even worse, on the stock market. I'm afraid the corporations won't stop until there's nothing left. And then where will we be for jobs?"

▶ 23 ANNIE HAULS

"WE WORK ON THE PREMISE THAT YOU HAVE ONE golden hour to get a patient to hospital. On an island like this, that's a real challenge – basically we just have to scoop and run."

Annie drives ambulance on Galiano Island, in the Outer Gulf Islands of British Columbia. She also runs a small trucking business, hence the trade name. Island garbage used to be dumped in a landfill site until it was closed by the owner, a major logging corporation. "Another girl and myself decided to be the garbage collectors, just for a while, until the islanders could sort out what they were going to do next. But people got used to the service, so a little business was born.

Now I've moved off on my own. As you can see by the name, I haul things, all kinds of things. The boys have their big dumptrucks, but when folks just want a pick-up load of topsoil, I'm right there."

She drives Brian and me to her favourite beach, warning us there may be a problem with the brakes on her old Ford pick-up. The road to the beach is a roller coaster. Descending each hill through galleries of trees, Annie pumps the brakes, gears down, and we hold our breath.

Montague Harbour beach is a broad sandy cove backed by arbutus trees, tawny-skinned after shedding their bark. Eagles soar high above in lazy, majestic circles. Odd tiny eruptions in the shallows turn out to be clams. "You can eat them," says Annie, "but you have to be careful of the red tide." She's referring to a highly toxic plankton that the clams absorb. Annie was born in a remote corner of northern Ontario, her mother having been taken to hospital on a railroad push-car. "I was used to isolation. When I had to go off to school in a town with a few thousand people, it was a huge shock. I was a real tough, got into all kinds of trouble – finally I got expelled. Then I was put in a Catholic boarding school, but I got into alcohol and drugs; the nuns caught me and kicked me out. There was a lot of torment in those years."

We watch a seal cavorting just off the beach. "For as long as I can remember I wanted to be with women, any way I could. As a child you don't think that much about sex; all I wanted was the presence of women, inside and out. But I really tried with men – I must have had more of them than Madonna! – but I was never happy. With men I never had a sense of dignity."

At nineteen Annie left home, to live for a few years in the Northwest Territories. At twenty-four she returned to visit her family – and fell in love with a local woman. "Up to then I'd only known what pleased men, but very little about the needs of my own body. Over the next three years, that's exactly what I learned. It was amazing." She moved to Vancouver, into other relationships. "Through all of that I was still drinking. But I also had this hunger, this drive to *show* people what I could do." She went to Spain to paint, but flew back to see her father, just before he died. "I think it's one of the reasons I drank, it was about the only thing I had in common with him."

A small deer approaches, kicking up little splashes along the edge of the water. "Something's wrong," says Annie, suddenly tense. "Normally she wouldn't ignore us like this, she'd be much more cautious." The doe's head droops, her swollen flanks heave. "I think she's pregnant. And she's exhausted – something must be after her." The doe continues her laboured flight along the beach. Annie asks two passing girls if they've seen any dogs around. No, they haven't. "I'll bet it's dogs," she says. "People think it's so wonderful to have a dog, but if they don't pay attention some of them run wild, in packs, and they go after the deer." The doe turns at the end of the beach and is gone.

In 1987 Annie came to Galiano Island for a visit and was enchanted by this little chunk of paradise. Realizing that to stay here she'd need some skills, she returned to Vancouver for a couple of years, studied fine arts, and took courses in welding and bartending. She also joined an AA group. "*Wow!* That's what it was like the whole first year in AA, just – wow! Since then it's levelled out. This year, the fifth, I'm thinking ain't life grand, and who knows what next year will bring."

Driving ambulance, she sees things that others don't, or won't. "I tend to be pretty forward, so people talk to me. A few of them have come to me with situations of child sexual abuse. One girl actually tried to commit suicide several times after she was abused by her uncle – I happened to know this man. You also learn to spot the results of wife battering. People don't like to think that kind of thing can happen here, but it does. That's why I got involved with the ambulance, so I could help and be a witness." A group of ambulance drivers, teachers, and school-bus drivers organized and got funding for a crisis support team. "A lot has changed since then," says Annie. "There's a lot more awareness now. It's much harder for these things to go by unnoticed."

Despite the impact she's had here, Annie Hauls' place on this island is far from secure. Only fifty minutes by ferry from Vancouver, Galiano has attracted people looking for weekend and retirement homes. For inhabitants like Annie on modest incomes, the price of housing has soared beyond reach. She rents when she can, borrows, house-sits – one way or another she hangs on.

"This is where I belong. And maybe one of these days I'll find a woman to love. I do believe it will happen. Who knows, maybe when I'm about sixty-five?"

III

Family values

▶ **24 SPRING**

AT FIRST LIGHT WE'RE CALLED AWAKE BY THE BIRDS, A little earlier each day. Most are on their way north, but stop over, lured by our feeder – orioles, rose-breasted grosbeaks, cedar waxwings, goldfinches, and the more familiar nagging chickadees and blue jays. A quartet of glossy cowbirds natter in the elm behind the garden, the males strutting their stuff – Choose me, Choose me! The woods are carpeted in wild flowers, the trees froth with pale green buds.

Behind Brian's shop, two robins build their nest in a discarded bookcase, low to the ground. Robins do not seem sensible to me. If Willy the cat discovers the nest – and how can he not on his regular patrols? – or a raccoon for that matter, those babies will be canapés. We check the four eggs daily, while Willy sleeps. Finally they crack open. The little bald heads are all gaping mouth, waiting to be fed.

Their down comes, then feathers. One day they're gone, all four of them. We look suspiciously at Willy, but *he's* not talking. We hope for the best.

Up close, turkey vultures are not pretty, but in flight they're magnificent, wide-winged, soaring in effortless spirals on updrafts from the bay. Today I see three of them, two smaller ones and an adult. It's a flying lesson. The young ones flap and flap, lose height, flap and flap again – it looks like hard work. The adult sails serenely, close by. I'm sure I can hear her whisper, Less is More, my dears, Less is More.

I'm thinking about family. And Family. Family with a big F is big business these days, and it's making careers for many mediocre and unprincipled politicians. Often the ones who speak most vehemently of protecting the children are the same ones who, driven by their own greed, are most actively engaged in making life on this earth hell for those who will follow.

I never felt I belonged in my particular Family. And I wonder, did any of the other inmates? Toward the end of her life my mother told me she'd been sexually molested by her father. He whined that she wasn't as friendly as her sister. That's Family. At the least sign I might be thwarting my grandmother's will – which I was expected to read from moment to moment – she would hit me full force across the face. In those days she was a powerful woman, and throughout my childhood I suffered from severe earaches. I still flinch when anyone makes a sudden move near my head. When I grew strong enough to fight back, my grandmother recruited my mother to hold me while she beat me with a hairbrush or rubber strap. My mother never dared refuse her mother, not even for the sake of her son. That's Family.

So what constitutes our family then, our small-f family? Brian and me? Why not? Together fifteen years, we are each other's next of kin. Each of us knows the other's strengths and weaknesses better than his own. At his father's wintry graveside, surrounded by Family, I took a breath and rested my hand on Brian's shoulder – why not? At my dying mother's bedside, when the minister asked who was who,

Brian said, "Mollie is my mother-in-law." Normally we don't use language like that, but in the moment it seemed exactly right.

Yet we're leery of winning points simply because we're so good at aping the Nuclear Family, the two of us and our two pets. These days many of us who have partners, and job perks like pensions and private health plans, are devoting enormous energy to winning spousal benefits. Two year ago my writers' union came around, and about time. We deserve the same rights as heterosexuals, no more and no less.

But something about it grates. In these dark ages when public pension and health care plans are being smashed by psychopaths in suits, when for the sake of the insatiable few more and more of us have no jobs at all, let alone perks, when so many of the world's people are starving, is it right that some of us should gain advantage *because* we're coupled, regardless of sexual orientation? Self-interest may be the fastest growing religion in the "civilized" world today, but ultimately it serves no interest at all, not even a healthy self. Whatever happened to what used to be called the family of man, or let's say humanity? Our family includes a few good relatives and a few good friends – gay, lesbian, and heterosexual – who've seen either of us, and vice versa, through major hardships and triumphs, also through the daily grind in between that comprises most of living. Isn't that what family is for?

Our family also embraces the animals. From nearby farmers we adopted a second dog, a big baby named Penny. They lived on a busy highway, and feared she'd be hit. Only six months old, she was enormous but determined to be a lap dog. She chewed pages out of the book I was reading, and the face off Brian's alarm clock. She was infuriating, and a joy. One afternoon she galumphed across the road on some urgent dog mission, and a truck going much too fast slammed into her.

We had the body cremated, and buried the ashes when the ground thawed, where Penny liked to run. I cried for days; so did Brian; we went over and over the same guilt-soaked ground. We should've watched her more carefully. We should've kept her tied up – but what kind of a life would that have been? Over and over.

Out for our morning walk, suddenly I spot Smudge running full tilt, low to the ground, her usually curled plume of a tail flat out. She's after a fox; it's less than a dozen feet ahead of her. I hope to God she doesn't catch it; a fox would be more than a match for her. And being the terrier she is, she would not back down. But what can I do? By now they're in the woods. If ever I could run like that, I don't remember it. Back home I wait, as helpless and full of ghastly imaginings as any parent. And then I'm just as pleased to see her home again, panting, hungry, wagging as if nothing had happened.

This is the time of new life. It's also the killing season. Much as we delight in Willy's imperial presumptions, this time of year we dread his nights out, after which we often find his mangled playthings here and there. He doesn't discriminate – mice, moles, frogs, any little thing that moves. It seems intolerable to let the half-dead victims linger in agony. So with a rock or a stick one of us will finish them off – please God don't let me miss the first time. It leaves us with the queasy feeling of being an accomplice at murder. We bury the little bodies with respect.

Spring rains have filled the pond across the road. As we approach it, me and Smudge, a pair of mallards erupt from the water, quacking their outrage at being disturbed. Frog love songs quiver in the air like electricity got loose, subside as we get closer, then sink into silence. I guess it's a privacy thing. The pond's surface is lightly feathered, a soft wind made visible.

All of this, if it's not family, what on earth is it?

▶ 25 IN THE BEGINNING

C

HE PHONED NEAR MIDNIGHT; WE'D ALREADY GONE TO bed. Hardly above a whisper, he told me he'd waited to call until his parents were asleep. He'd seen my letter about the book in *Xtra!*, the Toronto gay paper. He'd lived here all his life, and he wanted to tell his story.

Next day he didn't have to work at the convenience store, so he dropped by the house after school, in a borrowed truck. Cool clothes, glasses, hair. Cool attitude, or careful. Telling your story for the first time, and to someone who's writing a book, is a brave thing to do. C is seventeen.

From grade six on, he knew he didn't fit. "I wasn't interested in what the guys were doing, I just wanted to play house with the girls. And I had this huge crush on my grade six teacher; I couldn't take my eyes off him. I tried to change, you know, to be attracted to girls, but by grade nine I knew this was it, this is who I am." Since then he's taken steps to express who he is. "I told my mother last year I wanted to get an earring. She said no way, but I got one anyway. One day in the car she suddenly noticed it. She stopped the car; she practically screamed at me, 'I don't want a fag for a son!'"

C has actually worn a pink triangle t-shirt to school, an act of amazing courage. "When people ask what it is, I say it's an AIDS thing. They seem to accept that." Is he harassed at school? "Every day. Going to the library's the worst. The studs hang out in the entrance hall there, and when I go through they'll say 'fag' or 'queer'. Sometimes I ignore it, sometimes I come back with something like 'And your point is?' Of course if I ever approach one of these guys alone, he's scared shitless." In the boy's washroom, a list of names including C's is scrawled on the wall, under the heading FAGS. "The janitors just leave it. So I took an indelible magic marker and drew pink triangles all over the wall." These the janitors removed.

One day, just inside the school door, "A guy who's bothered me before threw me up against the wall and started beating me up. There was a crowd watching through the glass doors. A teacher walked by, but he didn't do a thing." Did he see what was happening? "For sure," says C. "The principal suspended the guy who attacked me. He said I should press charges, but I didn't. A few of my straight male friends said they'd get the guy, but I told them no. I'm not into violence."

C wants out. "This place is Alcatraz. I can't be who I am here, not a chance. I can't imagine why you chose to live here." Well, for one thing, I didn't grow up here. And it's beautiful, it's – he interrupts, "It's a hell-hole, that's what it is."

Where will he go? "To the city, where there's more of us and it's more anonymous. Everyone knows who you are here, and who you're related to. And I want a lover. I've only ever had sex with one guy. He'd have to be over thirty though; I'm not into younger guys." Why not? "All they want is sex. I'm not nearly as interested in that as I am in companionship. Older men have more to offer. And that's what I want. More."

Charlene

WHEN CHARLENE VACON'S UNIVERSITY ROOMMATE came out to her, "I told him he ought to be ashamed of himself, he was a sinner, he'd go straight to hell." Charlene is twenty-two, a graduate student in political science at Acadia University in Wolfville, Nova Scotia. Less than two years after that incident she calls herself an atheist, a feminist, and a lesbian. What happened?

"When I was eight," she says, "I remember suddenly getting this big rush over a girlfriend. I also remember how ashamed it made me feel. My parents are pentecostal. We all were, that's how it works. I thought about Jesus all the time; it was like having a shade over my eyes. And I knew that homosexuals go to hell. It just wasn't an option for me."

Charlene dated boys until her second year in university. The same week her roommate came out to her, "One of my professors came out, in class. I thought, Oh my God, what *is* this? But it did get me thinking, and within a week I'd admitted to myself that I was bisexual – partly because I'd got into feminism, which gave me a whole new way of looking at relationships with women. I have to admit though, the sexual part wasn't too appealing at first. Now I'm getting to like that more."

At university, Charlene is out – she coordinates the gay and lesbian group, works with the local AIDS committee, does interviews in the town paper. The home front, near Yarmouth at the south end of the province, was another matter. "Finally I had to come out to my mother – as long as I was hiding, there was this big void in our relationship. About all she said was she was afraid the church would disapprove. I said I could live with that. She doesn't accept my lover; she won't even say her name. On the other hand she did come with me on an AIDS walk, so she's trying."

For a while Charlene juggled sexual relationships with both men and women. Is she monogamous now? "Yes, but not by choice. I found it just took too much emotional energy to maintain more than one relationship at a time. But I don't like the idea of monogamy; I'm scared of slipping into the whole middle-class family thing with two cars and a white picket fence. That's too *normal* for me. On the other hand I do have this fantasy – a little house in the country with a nice garden and a dog." She laughs. "What am I supposed to do with *that?*"

Tammy, Tom, and Geoff

"I SPOTTED TAMMY FROM WAY BACK," SAYS TOM. "SHE was *so* butch." He squeals on the "so." "Why thank you," says Tammy. Geoff giggles. We're in Tom and Geoff's tiny apartment, up a rickety flight of wooden stairs tacked to the back of a store. It's early April; icicles are starting to melt off the roof. A relentless dance beat throbs on the stereo.

Now in their early twenties, the three of them grew up here in Kirkland Lake, a rough-and-tumble mining town in northeast Ontario, population about 13,000.

Just seven, Tammy informed her startled parents that she was half-girl, half-boy. "When we played house I'd always play the man – that felt more normal to me." When puberty hit, she realized she was checking out the girls instead of the boys. "I tried to hide it, of course. I'd have sex with men, but it was no big turn on. My emotional attractions were always to women." At one point she overheard her father say that if any son of his was gay, he'd shoot him.

By the time she was twelve, Tammy had started drinking, and by grade seven she was using drugs. "You name it, I used it. They're as easy to get here as candy." She's off the drugs now, still drinks, but less. "When I was stoned I could be anyone I wanted to be; I could hide from who I really was." In grade seven she slashed her wrists. At fifteen she deliberately overdosed on drugs. "But I think now that maybe I held back a little. I couldn't stand the thought of leaving others with all that pain."

In grade ten Tammy met Kelly. They moved in together, both drinking and doing drugs. "We didn't have any gay or lesbian friends. We never went out; we just kept to ourselves." Then they saw an ad in the local paper; two other lesbians in town were looking for contacts. "We couldn't believe it. We cut out the ad and hid it – we were much too scared to answer." Finally the four of them connected by phone, and then they met. "They had all these amazing books about lesbians and gays. We just *devoured* them."

Last year Kelly and one of the other lesbians became lovers,* and the two couples broke up. "Here we'd just managed to create this little community, and suddenly it all fell apart." Someone talked, and the news got back to Tammy's mother. "That was it, I was out." Without a word, her mother handed Tammy a card. "I was afraid to read it. But all she said was I'm sorry the relationship didn't work out. The card was even signed by my dad."

By the time he was twelve, Geoff was having sex with other boys. A year later he acknowledged in a letter to himself that he was gay. Searching his room for drugs – "I never touched them 'til I was seventeen, and even then I didn't really like them" – his mother found the letter. Angrily confronted, Geoff denied that he was gay. "I went right out and had sex with a girl, just to prove I was straight." Then he was raped, by a janitor at the high school. He told no one. "I was a loner anyway. I got into the drama club, but mostly I just stayed home."

Because Tom had been having sex with his girlfriend through his late teens, "I figured oh no, I can't be gay. But I started to notice it was the Chippendale [male models] calendar on her wall that was really exciting me." A school trip to Toronto provided a tantalizing

---

* More on them in Ch 57

glimpse into the urban gay scene, and a couple of close encounters at the swimming pool back home confirmed it; yes, he was gay.

He and Geoff had been drama club buddies in their early teens, then their friendship lapsed, Geoff being four years younger. But Kirkland Lake is a small town, and their paths kept crossing. Finally when Tom was twenty-one and Geoff seventeen, they renewed the friendship. It turned quickly into mutual courting, and they became lovers. Tom was the first person Geoff ever told that he'd been raped.

After he'd go to bed at night, Geoff would climb out his window, leaving it unlocked, and go off to meet Tom at the video store where he worked. He'd climb back in the window just before dawn. One morning he returned to find the window locked. He left his parents a note saying he was sorry he'd been so much trouble, and hid out in Tommy's apartment.

At school, the vice-principal demanded to know why Geoff had been missing class. Geoff told him – this was the first adult he'd told that he was gay. Within days the news had spread through the school. Geoff was taunted, called "fag," "queer." One day in drama class, "Suddenly the lights went out. I heard 'fuckin' faggot,' I got punched in the face, and then the lights came back on. I didn't go back, I just quit school."

Meanwhile Tammy and Tom had been checking each other out at the video store – both wore pink triangles. Soon the three of them became friends. They agreed that Kirkland Lake didn't have much to offer lesbians and gay men. "In North Bay, Timmins, or Rouyn you have groups and dances," says Tammy. "You can have a normal evening out with your friends, without worrying about getting yelled at or beaten up like here." Tom adds, "But if you don't have access to a car you're stranded." Finally they concluded that if they wanted a group, they'd have to create one.

"We got a P.O. box and we put ads in the local and regional papers," says Geoff, "as well as on the cable TV – Tommy's grandfather owns it." Tom: "Each of us will reply to each of the people who writes us. If they give a phone number we'll call. If they give a full name, so do we." Tammy: "Sometimes we'll tell them quite a lot about ourselves. We want people to feel they can trust us." Geoff: "We've even met a few of them, and one or two have become friends."

But just as this embryonic grouplet is being launched, two-thirds of its crew are ready to jump ship. Tom and Geoff are heading for Toronto. Geoff: "I want to go back to school, and I want to see what it's like to live where there's a real gay community." Tom: "I've been eleven years in the family business here; I don't want to be stuck in it all my life." Geoff: "I've never been anywhere. If I don't move now, maybe I never will."

And Tammy? "Oh, I can see why people would want to leave here. But I think I'll stick around for a while. I have a job; I'm accepted by my family. Of course I get a kick out of Toronto, it's sort of like a feeding frenzy down there. But I'm always glad to get back. I like being out in the bush, I love to fish. Who knows, maybe after a while Tommy and Geoff will get tired of the big city." Tom: "I don't think so." Tammy: "We'll see." Geoff: "I really don't think so." Tammy: "Uhn-hunh...."

▶ 26 MODERN PARENTING

Dennis

"AT SCHOOL, SOME OF THEM WILL SAY THINGS LIKE 'YOU got a gay dad, you're a fag,' and stuff like that. I just tell them get a life. You can't let things like that bother you." Jordan is seventeen. I'm sitting in the garden with him and his father, Dennis, on a warm spring day. Jordan is standing, fretful, here and not here. They live in Dawson Creek, in northeast British Columbia. Looking down their street you can see the prairie at either end. This is Peace River country, in late May.

Dennis scolds Jordan for leaving his bike in the drive. "How many times do I have to tell you...." They argue back and forth; then Jordan is gone, and for the moment the bike is out of the driveway.

His mother is a lesbian in Vancouver; he goes to her for the holidays. "We told him about us when he was nine," says Dennis. "Sometimes he'll use it as a weapon against me – they'll use anything, won't they – but by and large he's pretty accepting." Except of his father's smoking, which is heavy.

Dennis is forty-one. His long dark blonde hair is pulled back into a pony tail, streaked lighter by the sun. "I spend as much time as I can out here in the garden. We have such short summers, but nice long days." Dennis grew up a few miles from here on a farm; his grandparents were among the first white settlers in this area. "I've been attracted to men since I was a child. One time on the schoolbus my brother got all of them to call me Mabel. It hurt for a while, but then I told them since Mabel was a dull name and I wasn't, they better call me Maybelle." He chortles.

At eighteen he moved to Vancouver, and dove into the downtown gay scene. "I kept looking for a relationship just like my mother and father's; it was conditioned into me that that's what you were supposed to want." He married a lesbian who also wanted a child. Jordan arrived, the parents split, and Dennis became a single dad. The two of them went off to Jamaica. There Dennis married again, and the whole gang moved back to B.C.– Dennis, his new wife, her three kids and Jordan. "After seven years of that, I just quit fighting it, I finally accepted that I was gay. It took me that long to unprogram myself." He moved north with Jordan.

In the morning, Dennis fusses over his son's lunch. "Will you relax?" says Jordan, "I'll survive." "Not on chips and coke you won't, not if I have anything to say about it." They natter at each other, Jordan half out the door. Then Dennis and I cross an open field, leaning into the sharp wind, to his class at the community college – Psychology 213. He and twenty others, mostly women, are learning the stages of child development. Dennis plans to go on to university, to become a counsellor. "I don't want gay kids to have to go through what I did."

He's out to his immediate family. "I don't expect my mother or anyone else to tell me how to live my life," he says. "Not at my age."

She does exactly that, when she comes over to lend him her car. They argue, non-stop – is it genetic? But in the end it all seems fairly harmless. "One of my brothers thinks I'm out to lunch, and the other one pretends I don't exist. They've got that small man syndrome – you know, when you're a man but you're quite small?" He winks.

He knows of men who've left Dawson Creek because there was neither health care nor support here for people with AIDS. "I wanted to do something, so I set up an AIDS awareness table at the mall. Some of the people thought it was Farm-aid, raising money for poor farmers! I also got the health unit to finally put out some safe-sex information. And I've done interviews on a couple of TV and radio shows. I even got some money to get a group going, but no one would help. It makes you wonder sometimes why you bother."

Why does he? Why do they stay here? "Well, there's my course. Jordan has friends here, and my mother's just up the road. Plus it's too expensive to live in the city, and I don't happen to think it's any place to bring up a kid."

That's the parent talking. What about Dennis, what does he want? "Me? A relationship. Of course it's nearly impossible to find compatible people in a small town like this, so many of them are in the closet. And there's nowhere to meet. You have barbeques and private parties, but most of the people there will be straight. When it really gets to me I put a For Sale sign out on the front lawn. Anyone interested? I'll throw in the bike."

"Woody"

"WHEN MY SON WAS FOURTEEN HE SAID TO ME, 'ALL FAGS should be lined up and shot.' 'Oh?,' I said, 'and what about me?' 'Not you,' he says, 'you're different.' 'But I'm one of them, how can I be different?' 'Well,' he says, 'you're my mother.'"

"Woody" lives in Grande Prairie, a small city in northern Alberta. She's fifty-three. She grew up on a ranch in central B.C., riding, hunting, and fishing. "When I saw what the choices were, I wanted to be a man, who wouldn't. I hated inside work; I wanted to be a protector of women. But I just assumed all that would pass. Girls got married and had babies; that's the way it was." At seventeen she married, they moved north, and she had five babies. Like her parents and her husband, she drank. "For me it was a cover; I could always say I didn't know what I was doing."

By her early thirties Woody was sleeping with women. "When I told my husband, he told me to go for it. He'd tried with a man, and he thought he could handle it." At thirty-three she left him. "By then we were fighting, *really* fighting, hitting each other – that was no way to bring up kids." She joined AA in the small town where they lived. Her sponsor advised her to move to Vancouver, where she'd find a gay AA group. She moved, found such a group, and quit drinking. Then she found a lover, and started drinking again. "I didn't see how I could manage without the booze – it made me so much looser and easier to get along with." There were other lovers; the last one died of cancer in 1991.

How did her children deal with all this? "They blamed me for pulling out of the marriage. And they really resented it when my partner would tell them what to do. I felt pulled all the time, between my kids and my lover. They also had some hard times at school; they'd get called 'lez' and 'fairy' – I think maybe they started to see how society discriminates against us. And over the years they've watched me struggle with alcohol and come through that okay. I've changed a lot; so have they." Even the would-be fag-shooter? "Him too. All of us."

In the mid-'80s Woody went through another major change. "When my father moved off the reserve to buy land, he lost his status. We never talked about it much, and I never thought about being an Indian. But one time when I was pregnant I went into this restaurant for a glass of milk. The owner said, 'Show me your money first.' I was *so* hurt; nothing like that had ever happened to me before. It made me start to notice how much prejudice was out there." When federal law changed in the mid-'80s, Woody applied to regain her status. "It seemed right to me that we should stand together, hold our heads up and take our rightful place. It was like coming out."

Recently she joined the local gay and lesbian group here in Grande Prairie. "I'm the only woman. It's funny; I feel like the mascot." They have tried to recruit other women. "It's hard. Gay women tend to stay home here. You have to watch yourself all the time when you're out in public, you can't touch, you have to be careful not to say the wrong thing. So if women want to go out, they go to Edmonton." It's a trek, four hours drive to the southeast.

Woody's a grandmother now. All but one of her children have left home, and at nineteen the youngest is on her way, touring with a native dance troupe. Woody's next move will be to a larger centre, where she can train to become a drug and alcohol counsellor. "I'm looking forward to being in a place where I can just be who I am."

We're often accused of recruiting. It seems Woody's kids have taken over the job. "Now they'll say to me, 'Hey, Mom, look at her, she's nice, you should get to know her.' But I'm not ready for that yet. I know what I want now, and I'm not in a hurry like I used to be. I know there's someone out there for me. And I know that good things are worth waiting for."

Sean and Rick

SEAN'S LOG CABIN GOT STUCK HALFWAY UP THE MOUN-tain. Unable to negotiate the next hairpin turn, it stayed there for months, with Sean and his son living in it, perched on a flatbed trailer blocking the switchback road. The neighbours were patient. "But Etienne was only two, so it all got to be too much. We moved into a little cabin I owned down on the beach. I would sleep with Etienne on one side of me, and a rifle on the other – these two bears kept trying to break into the kitchen. Finally they did, and I had to shoot them." One of the skins is mounted upstairs, glossy black.

Sean, Rick, and Etienne live on the side of a mountain in the west Kootenays, southern British Columbia. Up the same road where the house got stuck, I find Sean and Rick planting potatoes and flow-ers, in a light mist that blurs the snowy peaks. Etienne is staying with his mother this week. The house is a rough-hewn work-in-progress, inside and out. The ancient Volkswagen bus that got Sean here serves now as a chicken coop, full of peeping chicks. A high fence surrounds the vegetable garden, to keep the deer out. And the rest is woods.

Fifty now, Sean grew up in Québec. After a spell in a commune and travels in Europe, he heard of a small Quaker community at Argenta, B.C. He'd attended Quaker meetings since university. Living in Montreal by then, he loaded up the VW bus and took off. "I just thought of it as another step; I really had no idea that I might stay." Someone offered him a log cabin, and he decided to haul it up the mountain where he'd bought a piece of land – why not? It took a year.

"As I grew up I formed relationships with women, but I was also doing it with men, though I was quite careful to keep that a separate part of my life – on the side, as it were. Gradually over time, men seemed to move from the periphery to the centre." Meanwhile, Sean's partner, Lucie, became pregnant. "I was amazed, quite amazed at how happy that made me." But she had a miscarriage. "And I was devastated – I hadn't realized how much I wanted to have a child." Then Etienne was born. Sean and Lucie lived together for a few weeks, then agreed it would be better to live separately. Their son commutes between them.

Rick is thirty-six. Born in Germany, he grew up in Turkey, where his father worked at the embassy. At seventeen he left home to roam the world, and at eighteen he came out. "I was so relieved; it had felt so forced to be heterosexual." Back in Germany by then, "I got bored with urban life, and running all the time to the gay ghetto – there had to be something more than this." He was due to chaperone some German exchange students on their way to Calgary. "I put ads in a couple of western papers looking for rural gay men. Sean's letter was the nicest one I got. He said I could hike to his place through the mountains, but I should be careful of the bears. I showed the letter to my friends; we thought it was so amusing, so exotic."

He hitchhiked into the mountains, where snow still lingered in the high passes. He found the trail, did meet a bear – "I understood what it means to be scared shitless" – but on the fifth day he showed up at Sean's, just in time for lunch. "I stayed three months, went back to Germany, closed things up there, wondering all the time what the hell I was doing – and here I am."

That was five years ago. They've been working their way

through the immigration process. "There's no official policy yet on same-sex partners," says Sean. "They do it case by case. Among other things we had to give proof that we're a couple – financial documents, bills, that kind of thing." "We had lots of letters of support from people in the community here," Rick adds. "It would be really hard to do this if you were in the closet."

When Rick came out of the mountains, Etienne was three. "For a while there we were all quite tentative with each other," says Sean, "and perhaps Etienne was a little jealous." He's eight now. "I think it's changed his life to see two men so comfortable and loving with each other – this is a really important example, a whole new vision of what family can be."

In a community where virtually every lifestyle is an alternative, Sean and Rick feel quite at home. Sean: "There haven't been any problems for us or for Etienne – none that I'm aware of. People know us here; they accept us as a family." Rick: "Here in Argenta we can dance together at the square dance, no problem, but I don't think I would do that anywhere else – I'm too well trained as a gay man. Away from here, out there, that's the real world."

When Etienne was in kindergarten, the two of them took turns walking with him down through the woods to the tiny community school, and one of them would pick him up later. One afternoon it was Rick's turn. "That day one of Etienne's classmates, a little girl, said to him, 'Rick is your second daddy, right?' When I heard that, it made me feel very good. It gives me reason to hope."

▶ 27 TOTAL IMMERSION

JUST AS CAROL AND I SIT DOWN TO LUNCH A NEIGH-bour skids into the lane. The school-bus driver called him on the cell phone – the horses are loose; they're out on the highway! Mary's at work; the girls, at school. Carol jumps into the neighbour's truck; he's already got his horse trailer hitched on. They retrieve the horses, bring them home, and coax them into the corral. "Thank God none of them was hit," says Carol. "I just checked all those fences. Shows what a good job I did, eh?"

They live on fifty acres of steep, sandy land beside a river, a few hours west of Edmonton, Alberta. In late May the river is still swollen, tumbling with runoff from the mountains. The Rockies erupt in the distance, their peaks lost in cloud. Through a long, slow twilight we sit by the river, a fire warming our backs. The dishes are done, the animals fed, tomorrow's lunches made, the girls have done their homework and gone to bed. A deer browses on the other bank.

Mary is hesitant to tell her story. "I'm not much of a talker," she says. "It irritates me when people talk a lot but they don't really have anything to say." Carol and I persuade her that others may benefit from her experience. For example, what was it like suddenly to acquire a ready-made family four years ago when Carol and the girls (seven and eight years old) moved in? "Well, I'd always had pigs, sheep, or horses to look after. At first I couldn't help seeing the kids pretty much the same way." Carol laughs. "She still does, sometimes." Mary: "In fact if you want to go anywhere, it's harder to find somebody who knows how to care for the animals than it is to find a baby-sitter!" Carol: "Not that we ever go anywhere." Mary: "Well no, but if we did."

Carol is thirty-four. She grew up on a small farm, then moved to Edmonton. In high school she had a boyfriend and a girlfriend. At sixteen she left home to live with the girlfriend's family out in the country. "I played lots of games though; I also went with this fellow – until I got so mixed up I finally went home to my parents and just tried to be straight." And gave birth to two daughters. "Their father drank a lot – he still does – and he was quite abusive toward me. So we got out." Carol was twenty-three.

Mary is forty-one. She grew up the other side of the river, then bought her mother's "home place" on this side. At seventeen, fresh out of high school, she had her first relationship with a woman. "I've never really had any doubts that this is who I am." She'd meet women at the clubs in Edmonton, and held annual camp-outs here for her friends. Carol came to one. "It was all a bit too wild for me," says Carol, "but Mary and I were attracted to each other instantly." "It was weird," says Mary. "Just before that I'd been to see an astrologer, and she told me that a woman with kids was going to come into my life quite soon." After a year of courting, Carol and the girls moved in.

"We were so la la we just went ahead and made the move," says Mary, "but we were both kind of nervous too." Carol adds, "Especially about living with kids so close to a small town." Mary works at the local pulp and paper mill, and Carol gives voice lessons in town, to thirty private students. Carol: "We talked a lot about how to make things okay for the girls; we wanted to protect them from unnecessary heartache." Mary: "Basically we just wanted to be good parents."

Carol: "I really hated telling the girls to keep our relationship to themselves; that's the opposite of how I want to be in the world. But we found out pretty fast what can happen out there." Mary: "The first year they were here, a kid on the school bus asked Hailey if she knew what a lesbian was. She said no she didn't, but that really threw us for a while; we could see what they might be up against." Carol: "The adults do it too. The schoolbus driver asked my oldest girl if she lived with Mary. She panicked and said no. It really ticks me off when adults do that; it's so sneaky. I'm sure this woman already knew."

One day at supper the younger girl burst into tears. Grilled by a teacher that day, she'd admitted that her mother was a lesbian. "We nearly lost our supper," says Carol. "The next day I went in and confronted this woman. I told her my daughter really trusted her, and it would be a shame if anything she'd said to her in confidence about our family got out and affected my kids' education. She promised that it wouldn't. But just in case, I went to the principal, told her the whole story, and asked her if she heard anything inappropriate from any of her staff, please to deal with it."

For academic reasons Carol moved the girls to another school. Before the principal would agree to enroll them in French immersion, he wanted to meet her husband, to be sure he supported the decision. Carol: "I told him I had a partner, and I would have to see if *she* would come." Mary: "So I got dragged into the school for some chitty-chat. It all turned out fine. But I'm a bit of a hermit, and I have to admit I'm uneasy with Carol being out to everyone like that. I just have to keep reminding myself it really doesn't matter what people think; I don't have to explain anything to anyone."

Carol: "Having kids sort of forces us to be out. All in all that's probably not such a bad thing; otherwise we might just stay locked up here forever." A local minister asked Carol to start up a children's choir. She agreed, but on two conditions: she would not hide the fact that she's a lesbian, and the choir would be open to all children, regardless of religious affiliation. A few parents have grumbled about her sexual orientation – though never to her face – but the choir is so popular with the kids, no one has withdrawn.

By their separation agreement, the girls still see their father regularly. He tells them regularly that in God's eyes their mommy's relationship is a sin, and what they really need is a daddy. "In fact," says Mary, "they've both said they're getting tired of going there. Apparently all he does is drink, lose his temper, and fall asleep."

It's dark now, here in their valley. The fire has died to glowing embers; it spits tiny fireworks into the black velvet air. For a long time no one speaks but the river.

Then Carol says, quietly, "Sometimes you can get to feel kind of isolated. We wouldn't mind connecting with some other lesbian couples who have kids – you know, healthy people who like to be outdoors, go on pack rides, that kind of thing." Mary: "They don't absolutely have to have kids. I guess they don't even have to be lesbian. Just so long as they're not screwed up." Carol: "We wouldn't mind if our world was a little bigger, that's all."

▶ 28 BOOM

AT SCHOOL FOR A PARENT-TEACHER MEETING, "PIERRE'S" grade one teacher told Diane he's been learning to write sentences – for example, J'ai un beau petit papa. "Can you imagine him sitting there writing that?" says Diane. "What must he be thinking?" Pierre is six. Four years ago Diane adopted him from Haiti. They live in the Laurentian mountains north of Montréal, with Diane's partner,

Maud, and "Mimi," a two-year-old adopted Haitian girl. There are no papa's in sight, beau or otherwise.

No one's booked in tonight at the Bed and Breakfast. Maud has just fed the pigs. They're in the barn now, after a summer foraging in the woods, an advance clearing party for a field that's been half a century out of use. This afternoon Diane canned a year's worth of tomatoes and set herbs to dry on wooden racks suspended overhead. Tomorrow she'll harvest red hot peppers from the greenhouse, made of recycled windows, that opens off the kitchen. For supper we have organic vegetables from the garden, couscous, and fresh plum cake with homemade yogurt and maple syrup tapped from the trees up the hill. Pierre is up and down, here and there. Mimi offers me bean sprouts from her plate, smiling and chatting away as if Brian and I were family too, like Luc and Jean-François, the two gay friends of Maud and Diane's who drove us here.*

Maud is forty-six. She grew up in the woods near La Tuque, in central Québec. "My mother always liked to knit; she still does at seventy-nine. As a child it was a dream for me to have sheep, so I could provide wool for her." The little that Maud heard of homosexuality was all bad. At eighteen, away at school, she had her first lover, a woman. She moved to Montréal, and got a job teaching outdoor activities at a CÉGEP (community college). At the same time she taught skiing in the Laurentians, helped other lesbian friends build their homes, and searched for her own dream place. Eighteen years ago she found it, 117 wooded acres on a hillside with no buildings. Within a year she'd built a log house, with an immense two-sided stone fireplace for heat, and many ingenious touches like hinged stairs that can be hoisted out of the way. Friends helped, and her father. Maud learned as she built.

Diane is thirty-six. Born at St Antoine in the lower Laurentians, she had girlfriends at summer camp, and boyfriends in the winter. "It was like having two completely separate lives. But those sexual experiences in the summer, they didn't seem like the real world to me. My

---

* More on them in Ch 19

Catholic background was so narrow, so closed, that I couldn't imagine anything else but getting married and having children. Also two of my sisters had babies quite young, so I was the one who had to be good, for the sake of my mother."

At community college in Montréal, Diane saw Maud's name on the schedule of classes. "My heart went boom; I knew this would be a very important meeting for me." Just from a name? "I don't know why, but the name carried the imprint of the person." Over the next two years they became friends. Diane: "Others thought we were together, but we were very naive ourselves." Maud: "I had to be careful; I was a teacher, she was a student – she was only seventeen."

One day in a class on community groups, Diane heard a gay man and a lesbian speak of their experiences. "It was the first time I ever heard it spoken, out in the air like that. I was amazed." Driving somewhere with Maud, she described the class, and her reaction to it. "After a while Maud said, 'That's my experience too; I'm one of them.' I nearly jumped out of the truck; I thought my God, they're everywhere!" They became lovers. Diane told a man she was also see-ing; he said it suited her. By the next spring Diane had moved into the partly built log house. Maud continued to teach, commuting an hour and a half to Montréal.

Diane: "She was older, she had money, and building the house was her project, not mine. I needed something for myself." With no prior interest in the subject, she took a brief course in gardening, from the perspective of its role in the web of life. "I soaked it all up like a sponge; I wanted to know everything." Diane worked in the vil-lage and at nearby ski resorts, saved her money, and went off to England to study for a year at a school devoted to biodynamics and the work of Rudolf Steiner. "It starts with the intention, the meaning in everything you do, whether it's with plants, animals, or people. For us farming is an art, a way of working with all the realms, all the forces of nature – physical, energetic, and spiritual. For example, when you work with animals, you learn a lot about pure emotion, how they express themselves, what they need to have a good life."

Diane used to hate thinning a row of young carrots. "I didn't want any of them to die. But then you realize that if they're crowded none of them can do well. For the ones that are left to reach their full potential, they need space. This is the kind of decision you have to make, but very consciously. Biodynamics trains you to see the purpose, the spirit in everything." Last week the neighbour who usually slaughters the lambs was unavailable, so Maud had to kill her first. "The first one is the hardest. But he was very gentle, very patient with me."

For many years, Diane wanted to have children. "I wouldn't have minded being pregnant, but that wasn't my goal. Also I thought it would be less of a challenge to my mother, and the people in the village who are just getting to know us, if I adopted instead. But I kept putting it off – we were so busy, and I knew it wasn't Maud's interest." Finally Diane decided it was now or never, whether Maud was ready or not. She chose to adopt from Haiti, one of the poorest countries in the world after decades of corrupt dictatorship, a country of broken families. Working through a Haitian lawyer, first she chose a boy. Why? She sighs. "That's the question. I grew up with girls, and I know lesbians who have girls – something can turn in on itself; it can become a closed circle. But I was completely unprepared for having a boy come into this world we'd made for ourselves. His way of doing things, with fists or kicking the wall, I have no experience of that. Sometimes I have to call Luc and Jean-François for a little advice on masculinity!" She laughs.

Pierre and Mimi are playing in the next room. "I've had to develop my own aggressivity a little, or he'd walk over me. It's good; it's a higher exercise." She laughs again. Pierre bounces into the kitchen, complaining that his balloon has burst. Maud says, "Mais ça c'est-ce que se passe avec des ballons." That's what happens with balloons. He shrugs, returns to play.

Maud never wanted kids, but knowing how strong the impulse was for Diane, she agreed to make room for Pierre. "It was hard. When he came I was the third person; he wanted just Diane, he wouldn't let me touch him. And sometimes I need quiet, I need my own place. You can't have that with a child, especially a boy." Diane: "When you've waited too long for something you get obsessed.

Things were so bad in Haiti, and moving here was so hard on Pierre, I gave him my complete attention. He was like a little king."

The two of them agreed that before a second child came into their lives, they would build a separate house for Diane and the kids. Through the winter they built another log house, and Mimi arrived last spring, one-and-a-half years old. Tonight the kids are sleeping in the loft at Maud's, up the hinged stairs from the kitchen, but usually they're at the other house with Diane. When Pierre calls out that he has to pee, it's Maud who goes. They've made their peace.

Seven years ago Maud quit teaching, and since then they've survived without taking on outside jobs. Bed and Breakfast guests sleep in three upstairs rooms built onto the barn, and eat here in the bigger house. They can help with the chores of the season, skate on the recently dug pond, hike, bike, or ski for miles through the valleys and surrounding hills, just now in their full Technicolor autumn glory.

The organic garden provides for the family, guests, and animals. As well as manure, the cow gives milk to feed the lambs, and for Maud and Diane to make into a variety of semi-soft cheeses. These age in "la caverne," dug into the hillside and shored up with wooden beams and concrete. The organically raised lamb, chicken, and pork are sold directly to friends. A dozen hens provide eggs. Diane makes homeopathic compost-building preparations for sale through the biodynamic association. At the moment the beams in the living room are festooned with drying catnip, destined for a pet shop in Montréal. Much of the floor is covered in squash and onions, drying for winter storage.

Maud: "Sometimes people at the Bed and Breakfast tell us they'd like to live like we do. But it's not so easy, you have to do so many things. I have my pension from teaching, but we don't want to use it up." Diane: "Almost everything we make we re-invest in the place; we're always building something. But after a while you get tired of living on small means – especially now with the children. We have to talk about making other choices. Instead of doing everything ourselves, maybe we have to hire someone now and then. You can't work all the time."

If we weren't here, they'd probably be spinning wool from their sheep, the wool of Maud's childhood dreams. She and Diane both spin, and Diane weaves on the loom up in the loft. Diane: "Sitting at the spinning wheel, it's like taking drugs. It's dangerous; we forget to go to bed!" Maud: "For me the best thing on winter nights is to read a good book. I love that." Diane: "But now that she spins, no one reads anymore. It's something the kids can do, too; even Pierre likes it. We're all crazy for spinning."

I feel compelled to ask about the upcoming sovereignty referendum. We've seen Oui and Non signs everywhere. Diane sighs. "A 'no' vote will leave us with the same situation we have now, it will seem as if the English have won again. But I don't think a 'yes' vote would be any better. The question is so complicated, neither a yes nor a no is going to solve it. What we want is a respect for our differences. Language isn't the only one; there are so many distinctions in a big country like Canada – that's part of its richness. If we want to live together we have to acknowledge these things. It's like Pierre and me. We're fundamentally different people, but at the same time we have a lot in common. To live in the same house, we have to learn each other's language, each other's reality. It's the only way; it has to be done."

▶ **29 FAMILY VALUES TOO**

"I WAS AFRAID OF HEIGHTS, SO THAT ELIMINATED JUMP-ing off the roof. The idea of drowning scared me less, but since I could swim I didn't see how I could sink. Also my church said if you commit suicide you go to hell – that belief may have saved my life. But just in case, I had a shelf in the basement where I kept a length of rope, and a bottle of turpentine to poison myself."

Denis Beaulieu lives in a low-rise apartment in Sault Ste Marie, a small steel-mill city at the north end of Lake Huron in Ontario. Thirty-five now, he was born in Timmins, northeast Ontario, father franco, mother anglo. Six years old, he watched some boys showering at a camp ground. "I was just amazed; I'd never seen anything like it – to be naked was a big taboo in my family." The boys noticed him, and one of them yelled, "Look at the fag!" "That's burned into my memory, excitement mixed with shame." In grade one he was called "sissy," "tapette," "fifi" – Timmins was a bilingual town. He'd been raised Catholic, but at eleven joined a fundamentalist protestant church.

By his early teens Denis was stealing gay magazines from the local book store. Then his brother discovered his secret stash. "I had to assume that now everyone would know, and on top of that I believed I was going to burn in hell." With Denis present, his dad showed the magazines to some visiting relatives. "Look what my son the minister gets up to," he said, and they all had a good laugh. "I don't think I've ever felt so humiliated." Around this time the suicide fantasies peaked.

At twenty Denis married. At twenty-three he had his first ejaculation. "What a wonderful experience; I thought I must be cured!" When his wife told him she was pregnant, "I was thrilled, I wanted so much to be a parent." It was a false alarm. Denis started getting male magazines again, buying them now, and in due course his wife found them. She harangued him about being a fag, and made him go to a psychiatrist, to get himself straight. The psychiatrist told him it was time he accepted that he was gay – it was perfectly natural. "That was the first time in my life I ever felt accepted for who I am."

He and his wife separated, got back together. Denis advertised for penpals in a gay magazine, and fell in love with one of his correspondents. "But he was too far away, and I still had so much shame." Suddenly his wife informed him she was a lesbian; she'd been having sex with another woman for some time. "After I got over being mad at her we were able to be buddies; we'd go to the gay dances in Sudbury together."

At twenty-five he came out to a few people at his church. They told him he had two choices: either give up homosexuality and seek salvation, or there could be no place for him in the church. He walked, but still yearns for that place. Why not a less repressive church then, say the United? "They deviate too much from the fundamental beliefs I hold," he says. He's caught between a rock and a soft place.

For years he'd wanted to work with young people. He saved and went to Toronto for training as a youth counsellor. On his first terrified visit to a gay bar, a man picked him up. They went back to Denis's place. "I'd dreamed of this for so long, I was thrilled just to be touching him. After he left I was so happy I cried." Then his ex-wife left town with the assets of their joint business, leaving Denis jobless, homeless, and without funds to continue school. He managed.

Now he's a youth counsellor with a social service agency in Sault Ste Marie. Some of his clients are amazed at his openness. "One of them was afraid I'd get fired if my boss knew that I was gay and that I was telling *him* [the client] it was okay to be gay too. It's very important for them to know there's someone who's been there, who understands what they're going through." It took him a while to be open with his coworkers. "I used to be really careful about 'cleaning up' my apartment before any of them came to visit." Now the icons, the beautiful men that adorn his walls, are not taken down for anyone. A bookcase in his office is devoted to books on coming out and living gay or lesbian. Denis has also written original pamphlets for distribution through the agency.

On his own time he runs a help-line; the phone is open twenty-four hours a day. For some callers it's their first contact with the agency. And he launched a penpal network for the region. "If you don't have access to a car, and you're scared to use the phone in case your parents find out you're gay, you can be incredibly isolated. The penpal network is a way of helping young people in that situation to get in contact with each other." I asked him if I could interview some of the penpals, but confidentiality is sacred. "Once they've made the initial contact through our P.O. box, that's it; we have no further contact that might put them in a position where they'd have to explain to anyone why they got this letter or that phone call. If they need us, they know where we are."

Early in 1994 Denis applied to become a foster parent. After months of delay and hedging, the Children's Aid Society finally admitted it had an unwritten policy not to accept gay or lesbian applicants. He argued that according to the Ontario Human Rights Code, they could not treat him differently from a heterosexual. The CAS said it would consider the matter. Impatient after more months of delay, Denis took his case to the local media.

Meanwhile, at work he was suddenly informed that he must no longer disclose his sexual orientation to any client, not even a self-declared gay or lesbian one. Young people are vulnerable, he was told, and he was putting them "at risk." "At risk of *what*, I asked, the risk of encountering a social worker who might actually understand them for a change?" No response was forthcoming; he was simply told to shut up. Denis laid a complaint against the agency with the Ontario Human Rights Commission. "This wasn't just about me or my rights, it was about the right of any young gay or lesbian person to get the support they need and deserve."

By the end of the year, burned out from fighting on two fronts, he took a leave of absence from his job and withdrew his foster care application from the CAS. "I was so agitated and depressed by then, I was in no state to take care of a child. I told them I'd probably re-apply after I'd had time to recover." If only all would-be parents were so thoughtful. He toured the province for a while, giving workshops for agency staff on growing up gay, and dealing with young lesbian or gay clients. The anonymous evaluation comments ranged from "Best workshop I've ever attended" to "You're a very sick man."

In due course the Human Rights Commission ordered the agency to apologize to Denis, and to adhere to the equality provisions in the law. He's back at work now, and can tell clients he's gay when-ever he feels it appropriate.

Working with a counsellor, Denis realized that his passionate fight on behalf of gay and lesbian youth was consuming his life; he had very few other interests to sustain him. For the time being he's cut back drastically on his board and committee work. "Now I'm say-ing, look, I'm not the only gay person in town, how about others com-ing forward and doing some of this work that needs to be done?" When other agencies try to dump their gay clients on him, "I'll gladly advise them and I'll give them resources, but they have to do the rest themselves. If they say 'But we don't know anything about gays,' I tell them it's time they learned."

In terms of other interests, Denis is restoring his 1979 Buick, a great burgundy yacht of a car. He's doing all the work himself. "It's a wonderful contrast to my career, which is so cerebral. This mostly requires muscle, and you actually get results you can see. By the way, if you think Canadian Tire is a Man's World, try a scrap yard sometime."

The Childrens' Aid Society informed him it had reworked its policy, and would now follow "the Toronto model," where children have been placed with gay and lesbian foster parents. Then it reversed itself again, and decreed that neither gay nor lesbian applicants would be accepted as foster parents. Denis hired a lawyer, and is taking the CAS to court, on the grounds that the Ontario Human Rights Code guarantees equal treatment for all citizens, regardless of their sexual orientation. The battle goes on.

Meanwhile, says Denis, "The Buick looks fabulous."

▶ 30 **THE FRONT DOOR**

"WHEN I VISIT MY BIOLOGICAL FAMILY, I FEEL LIKE I'M going into another country. My parents, even my siblings won't ask me anything about my life, they won't even ask about my lover. I think they're absolutely terrified to hear *anything* that might force them to acknowledge I'm a *lesbian*. It's amazing – my God, here I am forty years old, and I'm still fighting to be accepted by these people. It makes me aware of how lonely I can be when I'm out of my own little community."

Cathy's little community is a small group of women who share a wooded property about an hour's drive south of Winnipeg. On a rainy June evening, we're gathered for supper at Joyce's house, a light, airy place with windows running up the sloped roof. Cathy's work partner, Jill, is just back from Nova Scotia with a load of fresh lobster.

Present are: Cathy; her partner, Sandra*; Joyce; Jill; Mary, who has a house back through the woods; and Margo, the woman she's dating. And me. The place is humming with talk and laughter; you'd think these women hadn't seen each other in years.

Cathy built all or some parts of each house here, including her own and Sandra's. She lives here but works in Winnipeg, running a small home renovation business with Jill, who's also a carpenter living in the city. They work mainly for women.

Cathy grew up in a conservative Catholic family. "For all I knew, homosexuality didn't even exist. So I just went along doing what I was supposed to, until my mid-twenties when I got a job in a place where most of the other women happened to be lesbians. Of course I only found that out as I got to know them. And part of me really disapproved. Then I became lovers with one of them. It felt so healthy and loving, but even then I still couldn't bring myself to use the word 'lesbian.' All I could manage to say was I happen to be involved with a woman. I've seen lots of women in the same situation. It's like you want to explore this whole new world, but you're too scared to go in through the front door."

Her face registers pain; her voice is unsteady. "Sometimes I'm overwhelmed by how much self-hate I still have in me. I'm trying so hard to be out there, to be who I am, but then there are times I just want to hide from all the hatred. You know it's out there. I sometimes wonder if we have a false sense of security." Some people in the town nearby refer to the community here as "that lesbian colony," and it is not meant kindly. "We can laugh about these things, but you can't get away from them; they just eat away at you." She's speaking with effort now, and crying. "But if you let yourself have any doubts, any questions, it seems *bad*, as if you weren't being strong enough, or brave enough – you know?" Nods all round, we know it well. No one's tried to stop her, no one pats her, there-there, dear. Someone gets her a paper towel. Someone remarks what a good Catholic she is. Everyone laughs, Cathy too. This is family.

---

* More on her in Ch 17

Of course the wine helps, and the food – but there's such warm laughter among these women, and gentle teasing of an intimate sort that can only work when people know each other well enough to stay clear of the tender spots. Joyce: "We scrap like hell, but the object is absolutely not to hurt each other." Sandra: "We've come to the conclusion that we're stuck with each other, so we better work it out." Mary: "I feel like I'm learning a new kind of intimacy here, free of the usual heterosexual family thing. Here we can be all of who we are. Believe me, these gals have seen parts of me that very few people ever have." General hooting erupts.

In addition to their carpentry work, Cathy and Jill also give workshops in the school system and for children's groups. "Our primary goal is educate them about women in the trades, but sometimes we'll just talk about the trades in general, and sort of sneak in the woman thing. Girls – and boys for that matter – are taught so early what's appropriate for them to pursue, even to be interested in. We want to encourage them to develop skills that otherwise might have gone to waste." Joyce jumps in, "Cathy is absolutely fabulous with kids, you have to see it to believe it." A chorus of agreement from the others.

"Well," says Cathy, "we have fun, they have fun, and who knows what doors we may have opened. That's the point, isn't it – to open doors?"

▶ 31 A WALK IN THE PARK

A GAY LAWYER IN TORONTO DREW UP THE ADOPTION papers. Then his clients, Ted and Leonard, went before the judge. "This is a first for me," said Her Honour, "usually people are adopted much younger." Ted, the father, is sixty-three, Len, the son, thirty-one. "On the other hand," the judge continued, "it's entirely within the law. Normally I'd need the birth parents' permission, but in this case obviously not." "If you need my mother," said Leonard, "there she is." Cecile nodded from the spectator's bench. She's sixty-seven. "That won't be necessary," said the judge, and that was that. Outside the court, Cecile handed Ted a card. It read, "Congratulations, it's a boy!"

Now the three of them live together in Huntsville, a town of about 14,000 in the Muskoka cottage country, northeast of Toronto. The household includes Leonard's dog, Tasha (named after a *Star Trek* character), and Cecile's dog, Candy. Through further legal procedures Leonard assumed his adoptive father's last name, "Watson," and a new middle name, William. Says Ted, "The name change was for additional safety. Some people around here were starting to talk – if we were father and son, why didn't we have the same name?" Cecile adds, with a laugh, "Now some of the neighbours call me Mrs Watson. I don't correct them; it would only stir things up. I tell him [Ted] that he has a wife in name only!" She still calls her son Len, and so does Ted. To friends in Toronto he's Len, but up here he's William.

Throughout William's childhood, his alcoholic father, Donald, beat both Cecile and the boy regularly. Then Donald moved in with the woman upstairs, and Cecile and William landed on her sister's doorstep, with two suitcases. William was twelve. "We got nothing from him, no help, not even any interest. My mother had to support us kids on welfare and a little money from babysitting."

At school William and two other gay boys were targetted by a local gang. Gang members raped one of the boys, and beat up William and the other boy repeatedly. Cecile called the police several times, but they did nothing. William: "I thought if I stayed at that school I'd be killed, so in grade eight I quit. At my new school, I got right in with a gang; I drank and did drugs with them. You might say I joined the enemy."

William wears hearing aids in both ears. Is the impairment connected to the beatings by his father or the gang? "No one's been able to say for sure, but it seems quite likely. At school they thought I had a learning disability, until it occurred to someone to check my hearing. Now I can hear things I never heard before, like wind in the trees. It's wonderful."

His first sex with a boy was at age twelve, with a girl at twenty-one. "Mostly I cruised the parks. I just assumed I'd get married, have kids, and sneak away for a walk in the park now and then." Then one of his partners in the park suggested he check out Gay and Lesbian Youth Toronto. "I went to a meeting, and that was it, my closet door flew wide open." He was twenty-two. Cecile noticed a marked change in her son, and demanded to know what was going on. William told her he was gay. "Oh, thank God," she said, "I thought you must be in trouble with the police!" William burst into tears. "It was such a huge relief; I'd heard about these other young people who'd been thrown into the street when they came out to their parents."

Ted's passage was smoother, and more discrete. From about age ten he knew he was gay, but also that he had to keep quiet about it. He worked for a while as a mechanical engineer, then taught until he retired with a good pension at fifty-four. All his friends were straight, and he was out to none of them. He lived with his mother. "I'd invite various women to professional functions, you know, for cover. One day my mother said, 'Look, we both know you're better off with the boys.'" In his thirties Ted met Jim, and they lived together for twenty-two years, in Toronto, but entirely outside any gay community. Then Jim became ill, increasingly distant and moody. "He went for test after test, but no one would tell us what was wrong." Jim was also drinking heavily. One particularly troubled day Ted went for a walk in a nearby park, and there he met William.

William: "I was trying to end my relationship with an alcoholic who'd lost his job and was living off me. He refused to leave my apartment until some friends and I actually had to carry him out bodily. It was a very stressful time for me." Ted: "And I was going through something similar with Jim, so we were able to support each other." Over time the two of them became good friends, meeting regularly in the park.

By now William was driving a Wheel-Trans bus for the TTC. With a relatively secure, well-paying job, he decided to buy a house for himself and Cecile. "All her life she'd been taking care of kids – most recently my sister's – and I thought it was about time she retired and got some enjoyment out of life." Prices in Toronto were out of reach. "In my teens I'd been up around the Huntsville area, and I loved it here." He found an old house near the centre of town with a separate unit for tenants, which would help pay the mortgage.

Ted: "Since William was putting so much into the Huntsville house but still living in Toronto, Jim suggested he come live in Jim's and my apartment." But Jim was getting more and more withdrawn and unpredictable. Eventually Ted and William moved in with another friend. Suddenly Jim was taken to hospital, and within twenty-four hours he'd died in intensive care. Not being a relative, Ted wasn't allowed in to see him.

The connection between William and Ted deepened, and they became lovers. Ted put in a third of the purchase price for the house. Then he raised the adoption idea. "Until I met William I never realized I had such strong paternal instincts. Also I wanted to avoid the situation that happened with Jim in the hospital." William: "I'd also been prevented from seeing a friend in the hospital with AIDS because I wasn't related to him." Even more compelling to him was the fact that for years he'd been trying to fill an aching emptiness left by his father. He'd seen counsellors and therapists, but the void remained. "Now here was this older man who cared about me, and who was willing to give me a pat on the back for what I was making of my life." He canvassed his friends for reaction. Some were shocked, but others felt it was exactly what he needed. He agreed.

William: "Now we're father and son, we're lovers, and we're best friends. I suppose some people might call that incest, but who cares, we're happy." And they're secure in what may be the only legally sanctioned relationship available to same-sex couples on this continent. But how did Cecile react to her son suddenly taking on a ready-made dad/lover? "I always made my life the way I wanted to, so I expected my kids to do the same." They bought the house in Huntsville three-and-a-half years ago. We're sitting in its roomy old kitchen. Cecile lives here full-time with Candy, who's jostling for position with Tasha under the table. William, Ted, and Tasha commute between Huntsville and an apartment in Toronto, where William works four-day weeks.

The first winter here, William spread word via another gay

couple that he was having a gay Christmas party. To everyone's amazement, two dozen people showed up. That initial impulse has turned into a social group of about thirty, mostly men, who meet once a month. They were gathering at Divine Lake, a gay resort not far from here, until a German businessman converted it into a "straight but gay-positive resort." Until they can sort out exactly what that might mean, they're meeting in each other's homes. Cecile is always welcome. Ted asks her how she experiences a room full of gay people. "They're your friends and they're nice people. That's enough for me."

William would like to confront his biological father. Recently he's had several opportunities. "He's so small and frail now, I could easily pick him up and throttle him with one hand. But when I walk into a room and he's there, it's amazing, I'm still afraid of him. I go right back to being twelve or even eight years old again. My therapist said I should write it all down in a letter. I did that, but I can't bring myself to mail it. It's eight pages long, both sides. When I read it to Cecile and her sister, they both cried. I guess it's good to get that out. But I'd still like to ... I don't know. I really don't expect anything from him. But there's still something I want to say, or hear. There's still something."

▶ **33 NOTHING'S CHANGED**

IN 1949 THE ANTI-RED WITCH HUNTS WERE GATHERING steam on both sides of the border. Targetted were not only suspected communists, but also homosexuals. In the eyes of the witch hunters, they blurred into one great subversive menace. Most men and women who knew they were homosexual kept a *very* low profile in those dark days. But not Jim Egan.

"The Toronto gutter tabloids were printing all these hysterical stories full of lies about homosexuals. Finally after a particularly vicious one, I wrote a letter to the editor, attacking the article. My letter probably ended up filed in someone's wastebasket." But he kept at it, and a year later one of his letters was published. "I suppose it was the novelty; they were so amazed that anyone would dare to challenge them, let alone demand equality for homosexuals. After that you couldn't stop me." With a wry grin, Jim's partner, Jack Nesbit, adds, "And nothing's changed, you still can't shut him up."

Through the '50s and early '60s Jim poured out a deluge of letters, articles, and interviews, in a one-man campaign for equal rights. Jack: "I was a very private person, and I just hated all the publicity. When they asked him to do a TV interview, that was the last straw – I said either you give it up or I'm leaving." Jim did the interview. Jack left.

Three decades later, we're sitting in the dining room of their split-level home, on a quiet street in Courtenay, British Columbia. Like most towns on the lower inland coast of Vancouver Island, this one is in rapid transition from logging town to retirement mecca. Jack is sixty-eight. His back and heart both give him trouble. Jim is seventy-five, a little slowed but still clearly in one of the higher gears. Both are smokers. On their front door a sign proclaims, Thank You for Smoking.

James Egan was born in the east end of Toronto. He remembers hanging out in lacrosse changing rooms, crowded with naked men – "I thought I was in heaven." By thirteen he was fooling around with other boys on his street. "They enjoyed it as much as I did, but I learned very quickly you were *not* supposed to tell anyone. Of course I'd never heard of the word 'homosexual.' But by then I was already an omnivorous reader. I was reading something, either *The Picture of Dorian Grey* or Walt Whitman's *Leaves of Grass*, and suddenly I knew – that's me they're talking about."

If there are angels, one of them must have been watching over Jim Egan. "I never had any problem accepting my sexuality; I simply couldn't see anything to be anguished about." At twenty he told his mother. "She said, 'As long as you're happy, dear, that's all that matters.' As a child she'd lived in Monte Carlo, and gay people were just part of the social scene there – she couldn't see anything extraordinary about it at all!"

Jack grew up in Toronto too, with his own attending angel. "I was sexually active from about age sixteen, every chance I got. But I was a romantic, always falling in love with everyone I met." He dropped out of school in grade ten, took various jobs and then a hair-dressing course. After several brief affairs, at twenty-one he met Jim at the Savarin, an ostensibly straight but mostly gay pub in downtown Toronto. In no time Jim had moved into a small apartment with Jack – and his parents. Jack: "We were virtually in the next room, and I know we made lots of noise – but nothing was ever said. My mother just adored him."

In his teens Jim had worked summers on a farm. "I talked poor Jim into selling everything we had, and we bought a 200-acre farm." Jack: "I'd never been near a farm, not even for a weekend." They decided to raise pigs and turkeys, fell deep into debt, and moved to a smaller farm closer to the city. Jack commuted to a hair-dressing job downtown. By this time Jim's homosexual rights campaign was in high gear. Jack issued his ultimatum, and they split. Jim: "After three months of that I decided the relationship was more important to me than the politics. But I knew the only way I could give it up was to get as far away from Toronto as we could."

They bought a truck, loaded up their goods – including the five chihauhau's – and moved to Vancouver Island. There they found a house by the sea, and made their living collecting marine specimens for labs. When Jack's back gave out, they moved up the island to a "colony of left-over hippies" where they built a house and cleared land for Jack's beloved gardens. Along the way there were detours through the U.S., and in 1972 to India. Finally tired of moving, they settled in Courtenay.

Settled may not be the right word. After they'd been here a few years, Jim got elected for several terms to the local council. He approached it as he does everything, head on. "One night after a diffi-cult meeting I dropped in for a beer at the local hotel. I could see this little group of homophobes over in the corner. One of them yelled, 'Hey Jim, how about a blow job?' Well, over the years I've learned to think pretty fast on my feet. I shot right back at him, 'Thanks for the offer, but not tonight!' The whole place broke up."

Ten years ago, the two of them started a group for gay men in the area. First contact is usually made via a phoneline, which they advertise locally. After the two of them screen prospective members, they're invited to a monthly social chez Jack and Jim. "It's not for sex," says Jack. "If people happen to connect here, they can do whatever they like, but on their own time. We don't invite anyone under nineteen, and no dope is allowed."

Forty-seven years together; it's a long time. Are they monogamous? "For the first twenty years or so," says Jack. "Then we decided to open it up – as long as sex with another person didn't threaten our relationship, that's always been the rule. It had to be strictly casual." Jim: "Of course as we get older the field of opportunity narrows somewhat." Jack, with a grin: "He used to go for the young ones, but now he'll take anything up to seventy-five." Jim retorts, in mock outrage: "That is absolutely untrue!"

After all these years, Jim and Jack have been back in the news. The issue is the federal old age pension spousal allowance, available since 1975 to spouses who survive their mates. In this as in seventy-eight other pieces of federal legislation, "spouse" is defined as a person of the opposite sex, which effectively excludes Canadians in same-sex relationships. To a lifelong activist like Jim, the target was irresistible. "When I applied, Jack was sixty-one. Mind you, I didn't have the slightest illusion that we'd actually get the allowance. The point was really to launch a Charter challenge." The Charter of Rights and Freedoms guarantees that all Canadians will receive equal benefit of the law.

Backed by the federal court challenges program, James Egan and his lawyer went to court. At the first level they lost. The program agreed to fund an appeal, but a day later the Mulroney government cancelled the whole program. The lawyer working on the case offered to waive his fees, and they took it to appeal. And lost again. Then they appealed to the Supreme Court, and the historic case was accepted. The panel of nine judges heard the case in October, 1994.

Seven months later the judges, nearly all of them Mulroney appointees, handed down their ruling. By a unanimous vote they agreed sexual orientation should be added to the Charter, as a prohibited ground for discrimination. (This can only be done by an act of Parliament.) Then they split. Though several of them acknowledged that the law did indeed discriminate, by a majority of one they decreed that this was justified by history, and only heterosexuals need apply. In other words, the government was free to continue discriminating.

In Courtenay, Jack is gearing up to do some work in the garden. "I'm afraid I'm losing it," he says. "My health doesn't allow me to keep the garden the way I'd like. But – what can you do?"

Tonight Jim will attend a public meeting organized by local fundamentalists calling themselves Focus on the Family. The meeting is titled "The Myth of Safe Sex." The content is predictable. But Jim, the uninvited guest, has every intention of giving them hell.

▶ ## 34 THE GENTLENESS OF A RURAL CIRCUMSTANCE

MAY 2. JANE RULE AND HELEN SONTOFF HAVE JUST taken their first swim of the season. After a night of heavy rain, the water temperature in their pool is sixty-nine degrees fahrenheit. They are noticeably pleased with themselves.

They live in a nest of tall trees on Galiano Island, between the British Columbia mainland and Vancouver Island. They bought their cedar house in 1973. Says Jane, in her trademark gravelly voice, "By then we had so many friends and social commitments in Vancouver, we felt we were losing control of our lives." "We really didn't intend to live here," says Helen. "It was just to be a retreat." Helen took a year off her teaching job at the university, and they tried out island life. Jane: "It was marvellous – for my writing, and for Helen's piece of mind. Our lives were simplified enormously." Helen: "We found we could have much more satisfying conversations than the ones you'd have at a big party or an opening – here we could really talk, with people we cared for, about things we cared about." In 1976 they made Galiano their home.

Helen grew up in a village in New York state. Her father died when she was eleven. "It was a good place," she recalls. "My mother had interesting friends, and we grew up accustomed to lively dinner table conversation, music, and books." At sixteen she went off to college. "I always had friends, both boys and girls, but I never had what used to be called 'it,' that girls were supposed to have. I used to wonder if I'd ever get married, and my mother would say, 'Well, yes, women do.'" The man she married had had affairs with other men. "I didn't think of myself as particularly sexual. But I cared a lot for Herbert Sontoff, and I think he was grateful for me." Helen moved to the small college where her husband taught, and there she would teach as well.

Jane was a child of the Great Depression. Her father worked as a travelling salesman, so they were usually on the move. But summers they'd retreat to an isolated cabin in the California redwoods. "From the time I was three or four I was spending the whole summer essentially by myself. That's where I learned to keep my imagination company. And I think it's where I acquired a kind of detachment that's served me very well as a writer – from sitting for hours watching deer feeding in the orchard, or fishing, or watching cars go by on the other side of the river and thinking, they're on their way somewhere but I don't have to go anywhere, I'm *already here.*"

At fourteen Jane fell in love with a woman. "The relationship was only tangentially sexual, because she was married and felt guilty – but I had no doubt this was what I wanted." Jane is godmother to her first lover's three children, now in their forties. At nineteen she went to England to write, fell in love and lived with a woman, but found she couldn't write. Out of money, she returned to the U.S. and got a job teaching English, and biology of all things, at the same east coast college as Helen. The day they met, Hurricane Hazel swept in off the Atlantic, knocking out trains and power lines.

Jane: "At the beginning I was much clearer than Helen about wanting to be lovers, sexually I mean." Helen: "But I did love you." Jane: "Of course there was no support in those days for a relationship like ours." Though Jane came to know Herbert – "I actually got along better with him than Helen did" – after a while she could no longer bear to hover on the periphery of Helen's life. In 1958 she headed west to Vancouver, to write. "It wasn't a real city then, just two high-rises and a lot of wooden houses – but there were the mountains, and the sea, and the most extraordinary gardens – I was overwhelmed by it. I called Helen and said this is insane, what are we *doing?*" Helen came for a visit, and stayed. She and Herbert divorced. "Now he has a real wife," says Helen, "and he's very happy."

In 1964, when Jane Rule's first novel was published, the two of them were teaching at the University of British Columbia. Jane was thirty-three. "In our private social life, we were quite open. In our professional lives we'd neither deny nor come right out and say anything directly." Helen: "I remember you giving tours of our new house – you'd insist on showing them our bedroom with its *one* bed." Called *The Desert of the Heart,* Jane's novel tells, among other things, of a woman who travels to Nevada to get a divorce, and becomes lovers with another woman. "I had no idea what a public role it would give me, from then on. I'd been writing for ten years and published practically nothing – I'd stopped thinking about an audience. Helen was really marvellous with all the uproar; she said if we lost our jobs, we'd simply have to cope."

They kept their jobs. Jane became a successful, widely respected novelist, published throughout the English-speaking world. She also became an articulate advocate for lesbian and gay equality. After they moved to the island, Helen retired from teaching, and has continued to be a relatively private person. Has either of them regretted Jane being so publicly defined as a lesbian? "I haven't," says Helen. Jane hesitates. "I think sometimes I've minded the 'lesbian writer' label, in that it may have been a barrier to a wider audience. In fact the only label I *don't* mind is Canadian, because that one I chose myself."

The two of them are settled now in their living room, each with a cigarette and a scotch at hand. When they arrived on Galiano, they took their time making connections. Jane: "In town we used to move in quite particular circles, mostly artists and the university crowd. Living out here you find yourself dealing with a much wider range of people. Ultimately I think it's quite healthy when so many points of view have to co-exist." Helen: "At the post office, or when you're waiting for the boat, you're always running into somebody who you know has quite a different political opinion from yours, but that's no reason not to have a pleasant, open conversation."

Social interaction here usually turns on local concerns – the fire department, the ambulance, the current battle to save former timber lands from being turned into subdivisions. It may not always start out pleasant or open. "I'd had run-ins with the postmaster here. The man was a little dictator," says Jane. "He'd actually threatened people; he could have burned my mail. So – I made him a plate of cookies. The way I saw it, this was a frightened, silly man, and you had to deal with him as someone who needs help. In my experience, people have power only if we invest them with power. And in a small community like this you can usually give people what they want from you – your help, your attention, your money – but you have to say, I will do it on my terms, this is who I am. I think it's so important to do that, to divest people of the power of their prejudices."

Summer afternoons Helen and Jane open their swimming pool to local kids. It's a bigot's worst nightmare, that children will witness with their own eyes two people of the same sex in a relationship as comfortable and natural as the surrounding trees. Jane also teaches a bit, informally – young kids will drop by after school to be inspired for an hour or two. These two Galiano matriarchs also pay a lot more than lip service to community economic development. Helen: "Young people can only stay here on the island if they can find ways to support themselves. We do what we can to help out." They invest in local businesses like a second-hand clothing store. Their garden is tended, beautifully, by a young gay man who lives up the road. When they have to go to the city, but don't want to drive once there, someone else will do the driving. Says Helen, "I really prefer to be driven by someone whose eyes are still working." A young woman comes by once a week to clean the house. Jane: "The less able we are to cope with things, the more people seem to be available to help. We help them, they help us – I think that's how community ought to work."

This presence of the young is also insurance of a kind, against one of the most common and devastating ailments of age – isolation. Helen: "We followed the example of Hoppie, a woman who used to live here. She was very good at making friends, and as she got older she would make friends deliberately with younger people. Otherwise she would have outlived all her friends and been very lonely. We've done the same thing. We're very grateful for our young friends."

It's late. The dishes are done and put away, the table is set for breakfast. By each of their places sits a little dish of pills. Helen's heart is tricky, and Jane's arthritis has forced her to retire as a writer. "I'll still do short pieces now and then," she says, "but if I sit more than two hours at the typewriter the pain is unbearable. Anyway I believe I've had a good go at it. I've said what I wanted to say, and I don't like the idea of repeating things I've already said."

At this stage in their lives, are they nervous of living on an island, so far removed from medical care? Jane: "If you ask most people on this island if they aren't too far from a hospital, they'll say, 'I hope I'm far enough.' When you get old, what the hospital does is not what you want. In the last three years of his life, my father must have had ten operations, and all they did was deplete him and make his last few years that much harder to live."

She draws a distinction between the island hospitals and the big ones in the city. A few years ago when he was up for a visit, her eighty-eight-year-old father suffered a massive stroke. He was taken to the small hospital on the next island. "They treated him with great tenderness and care. Being from the U.S., my mother was amazed that no one did anything to him just to make a buck. After he'd been in a coma for four days, we asked them to take the IV out, to let him go, and they did. If he'd been at home he could've have gone on for months or even years like that, because it would have been profitable for the hospital." "Canada is so much more civilized," Helen adds.

"So you see, rather than our location being a source of anxiety," says Jane, "it's actually quite reassuring, the gentleness of a rural circumstance."

IV

Knowing our place

▶ **34 SUMMER**

DROUGHT. IT'S NOT UNUSUAL IN OUR COUNTY, BUT we've never seen anything like this.

The grass crunches underfoot, baked to a crisp. People who've lived here a long time remember summers when half the county was on fire, and all it took to get the other half going was a bit of broken glass lying in a field. Fearing the same this year, farmers mow their crops down early. Once cut, the hay can't come back without rain. The fields look dead, like vast scorched lawns. Even in our shady woods the earth cracks open.

The rain barrels run dry. Then so does the well. We have to get the well refilled with water trucked in from town, where they take it off Lake Ontario. After ground-water it's like drinking from a swimming pool. To keep our parched vegetable garden alive, we pump water from the newly filled well into empty rain barrels, then in the evenings when the heat has subsided we use a can with a narrow spout to deliver a ration of the precious liquid to each plant.

Every day we check the sky for clouds. On the radio we hear that rain is expected in Toronto. Bad weather, they call it. Poor babies, might have to take an umbrella to the office. Late one night I hear tat-tat-tatting on our metal roof. Rain, sweet rain! Half awake, I imagine dancing naked in it. But before I'm out of bed the tatting fades away. Nothing; a cruel tease.

Out in the dying fields I rage at the sky like King Lear, but with no storm. The sky remains blinding white, impassive, a blank screen for the murderous orange sun. No wind. Or a hot, dry wind. Or a hot, humid wind. With grim satisfaction we note that this is the hottest and driest June on record. Nights, we stew in our own juice.

Not surprisingly, the drought got me thinking about water. Without it, no life, not on this planet. And that got me thinking about love. Not the Hollywood kind, the real thing. Call it respect, call it compassion. Without it none of us can thrive.

From time to time people write hate letters to our local paper. Race rarely comes up; in fact it's conspicuous by its absence. But it's always open season on homos. Usually I let these poison pen letters pass by, on the theory that responding only extends a bigot's platform, since he – almost always it's a he – will surely feel compelled to respond to the response. At the same time I can't deny that fear is a factor in my restraint. This isn't *The Globe and Mail*; it's our local paper, and everyone reads it.

This time it was a retired Anglican priest, upset that sexual orientation was to be included in the proposed federal hate crimes bill. After linking us with drunkenness, adult-child intercourse, and pornography, and blaming us for AIDS, his letter concluded, "Parliament is faced with a moral and spiritual decision: either to vote with God against any express or implied approval of homosexual or lesbian behaviour, or to vote against God." Nothing new there. But for some reason – the heat? – this time I composed a response, checked it with Brian, and delivered it to the paper by hand before I could lose heart.

I wrote that for centuries religionists like him had used their god to justify their own bigotry, along the way "murdering countless innocents in their crusades and inquisitions, as well as providing handy theological excuses for slavery, for the conquest and genocide of native peoples on nearly every continent, for the exclusion of women from places of equality in church and society, and now for the campaign to deny lesbian and gay people the basic human rights that everyone should be able to take for granted in a civilized society." And all of this, I argued, was exactly why such legislation was needed.

Two editions later the reverend replied that if he was a bigot then he was in good company, since 65,000 Canadians had signed petitions against the inclusion of sexual orientation in the hate crimes bill, and the politicians better heed the popular wisdom. In the next edition I replied that on this fiftieth anniversary of D-Day, it might be useful to recall how the war began – in 1933 a majority of German voters decided the best man to lead them was Adolf Hitler. He was *elected*. So much for the popular wisdom.

He responded that I was being silly, such a thing could never happen here, and anyway "gay lifestyles are both wrong and dangerous." By now the exchange had got others going, including one man who said I'd "sullied the memory of countless Canadian and Allied soldiers who died in the true battle against Nazi Tyranny." My response was already half-formed before I'd even finished reading: I wasn't aware that all those people had died for the right to hate. And the odd thing about hate is that it has two victims: the hated and the hater, who cannot help but be poisoned by his or her own venom. Bigots seem to me sour, unhappy people who've been let down by the gods they worship – capitalism, patriarchy, God. If they were not so unhappy, how could they hate so much? All of this I wanted to say, and much more. But Brian counselled me to hold my pen. What if someone else was moved to speak out on our behalf, shouldn't I make room? I bit my tongue. I *was* starting to feel a little exposed.

Unprompted by us, a heterosexual woman friend wrote a letter to the paper. "By fostering this sort of heartless, mindless hostility," she said, "the Reverend is causing untold pain in a world that would be better served with love." In a lead editorial, the editor supported the inclusion of sexual orientation in the hate crimes bill, certainly a first for this paper and this county.

There were two phone calls on the machine, and a note in the mailbox. One anonymous caller, a man, said, "Thank you, Mr Riordon, it couldn't have been said any better." The other call came from a local real estate agent, a nodding acquaintance: "It must have taken guts to write what you did. Congratulations." The signed note was from a woman: "Words can barely express my vast relief that you have said so succinctly what I was feeling. From the bottom of my heart, thank you." I nearly cried.

It took the bigots a while to settle down, and I have no doubt we'll be hearing from them again. The drought went on too, for quite some time. But eventually the rain did come, not tat-tat-tatting this time but good old fashioned heavy bring-on-the-Ark soaking rain that healed up the wounds in the forest floor and set the beets and carrots to growing like crazy.

Isn't it amazing what a little water can do.

▶ 35 A LOW PROFILE

"I WENT OUT WITH MY FATHER FROM THE TIME I WAS about five. With the ocean being so warm in July and August, he had to check the nets as often as he could so the salmon wouldn't go bad. Some days we'd go out round the headland and it'd be blowing a gale, with waves taller than the boat was long; it was terrifying. My mother never wanted any of us to go to sea, she'd lost so many relatives to it."

The lilt in Steven Doyle's shy voice comes and goes, like a tide. We're only a stone's throw from Ireland really, on the coast of Cape Breton in Nova Scotia. His people came over 150 years ago, and settled here on a strip of rocky, wave-battered beach between the Atlantic and the mountains. "We've always been tied to the sea. I'm the first generation not to fish." Just as well, with the fishery dying.

Steven's a carpenter, doing construction and repairs from spring to fall in the national park.

"Growing up here, it was a sombre way of life," says Steven, "and very much dominated by the Catholic church." It's just down the road in the village of Ingonish where he went to school – St Peter's, grey stone, sombre indeed on a rainy late autumn day. "From as early as grade two I can remember having sexual urges toward other boys. But the nuns were always preaching against carnal sin, and I could hardly imagine a boy and a girl doing it, let alone two boys. I thought I must be the only one like that, so I learned very young to keep a low profile."

He lives in a little colony of Doyles, his brother next door, his sister and his parents with their own houses just beyond. Steven worked on most of the houses, and his parents helped with his. "We're like a commune. Sometimes it can be a pain in the ass, when you can't find a shovel and it's down in someone else's basement. But I can go away and leave my house with no fear that it'll be vandalized."

At twenty, hungry for a wider world, he went off to college in Sydney, down the Cape. "And there I met the threat I'd feared all my life – I was hit on by another man. I couldn't handle it. I quit, came home, and stayed by myself, in a little bubble filled with all these gloomy thoughts about sin and hell. I was sexually retarded really – the first time I ever masturbated, I was twenty-four."

Finally he found a priest in another town who offered him help, through counselling. Steven was twenty-six. They corresponded through the spring and summer. "I came to admire him so much, I figured this is the life for me. When he invited me down for a visit, before I had a chance to tell him I wanted to be a priest, he threw himself at me. I was so shocked I ran away. Then he wrote to say he only wanted my friendship, so I went back, and this time I gave in to him. While it was happening he made it seem right, but when it was over he dumped the same old Catholic guilt on me. It took two years of therapy to work through all that."

When the addition of sexual orientation to the human rights code came up in the Nova Scotia legislature, the local bishop ordered his parishioners to oppose it. When he gathered his priests for a regular meeting in Cape Breton last summer, a former parishioner stood outside in the pouring rain, a one-man silent protest. Steven's sign read: "Gay priests: speak out for gay rights!"

After things ended with the priest, Steven's mother sensed that something was wrong. "She opened a door for me, so I told her first and then the rest of them. It was hardest telling my father and brother, I suppose because they represent the male way. My father went kind of pale, but after a while he said he'd always felt he had two good sons and that was still the case."

At twenty-seven Steven decided it was time to check out the gay world. He moved to Halifax, entered university, and dove into downtown gay life. "Along the way I realized a lot of guys are real jerks. What kept me sane was knowing I'd be coming back here each spring to work in the park." One spring he came home with a degree in English literature.

His house is simple, uncluttered, and pleasant, with warm wood, plants, and impressionist posters. He lives alone, without a phone – he found it more a nuisance than a benefit. "I'd had more bad experiences out there than good, and I concluded I wasn't going to meet anyone who'd make me happy, so I might as well keep a low profile and be celibate – I figured I'd be the kindly old uncle type," he says with a soft laugh.

Last spring when his parents visited Halifax, Steven tagged along. He was introduced to a man who happened to have grown up in the same village. "John was the first person to be openly gay here, and he was terribly stigmatized for it. I can remember watching him being tormented in the schoolyard – that's when I first decided to keep a low profile. He got out of here as soon as he could. In fact when we met, I was a little afraid of him – those stigmas die hard."

They saw more of each other, became friends, and found they had more in common than the stigma. John had also been involved with a priest. When he still lived in the village, men would come to him for sex – "straight" men who work now with Steven. "More often than not, these are the guys that are the alcoholics and beat their wives." In time Steven and John became boyfriends. "He's interested in a long-term thing, and so am I. I wasn't too comfortable having him up here, since I'm still a little afraid of what my family thinks. But they seem to be warming to him. And for him it's the first time he's ever been able to come back to the village and see anything other than the hatred."

On a November night, the ocean's deep, surly voice rumbles up the hill, as waves a mile long and plumed with spray thud into the beach. Winter storms off the Atlantic can still set this part of the world back a hundred years, closing roads that skirt the cliffs, snapping power and phone lines. People will huddle by a woodstove, play cards, make music, and wait for it to end.

"I don't know how long I'll still be here," says Steven. "The outside world is always calling. And now there's John. After I'm laid off from my job this winter, I'll probably go to Halifax to live with him and his brother – he's a carpenter too, so we may set up a little colony of Cape Bretoners down there. But one way or another, I know I'll always come back here. I can't be away from the ocean too long. It's in my blood."

▶ 36 HEART

"I ALWAYS SAID, IF I EVER BUY A HOUSE WE'RE ALL GOING to get together in it and do whatever we want." In 1969 Pauline got her house, in a Timmins subdivision. "Every weekend we had card games, parties, a lot of fun. Taxis would bring the people – some of those guys were already dressed up, some would fix themselves up here – then the taxis would come back later to take them all home. Sometimes we had every taxi in Timmins at our service!" She laughs merrily.

Timmins was a tough logging and mining town – now it's a small city of about 50,000 – in northern Ontario. The neighbours were agog. A woman down the street started a petition campaign to get rid of Pauline, but very few would sign. "Most of them said, 'We get along with her fine, so you can shove that paper up your arse.'" And that was that.

Pauline is forty-seven, of Italian background. Her parents fought, bitterly. "Many nights I cried, I wanted so bad to get out of there." She spent as much time as she could with her grandparents. "From my grandfather I learned how to work with cars, the tires — that was his work. I told him I wanted to do something else; he said, 'We'll see.' When he was dying I told him, 'Okay, you were right.' He had this big smile on his face." So does she.

At twelve Pauline told her parents she was homosexual. "My mother said to my father, 'It's your fault!' He said it was her fault. I told them, 'Look, if either one of you can't accept who I am, as soon as I turn of age I'll move, I'll change my name, and you'll never hear from me again.'" Things got worse. "Anything went wrong, my mother would blame me. When I was fourteen she told me to get out. So I did. A couple of old people took me in, and I got a job." In 1965 she moved to Toronto with a girlfriend. She told no one where she was going.

As soon as she found work and a place to live, Pauline began to explore the city. "I figured since I was there, I might as well find out if there were more people around like me. It took me about a year to find a few places where I could feel comfortable — I'm happy-go-lucky, I just wanted a good time, no fighters. I met a lot of interesting people." She worked steadily, and saved enough to buy herself an old car and a house. "I know how to handle my money. Of course those days, draft beer was only twenty-five cents." Why a house? "Eventually I wanted to get Mum and the kids down to Toronto, so I could take care of them."

But not just yet. It took Pauline's mother a year and a half to find her. "She was crying on the phone; she said 'Your father needs you, you have to come home to work in the family business.' I told her point-blank I would not change for anybody, and I wouldn't stay behind a closed door." After three years in Toronto, she went home. Why? "Because I believed my mother was scared and she really needed me, and maybe if I was around my father would be easier on her. But I didn't know how I'd cope with the hate I had for him. It was a constant battle right up to the day he died. That's what he left me. I've had a rough life, but I try to keep happy."

These days Timmins has a gay and lesbian social/support group, and halls are rented for dances. But Pauline's place continues to serve as an informal drop-in and party centre. We're in her basement rec room now, a small circle of lesbians and gay men, plus an assortment of dogs. Says Micheline, "Pauline will do anything for you, and she never asks anything in return. There's not too many like that around here." "It's what I learned from my grandparents," says Pauline. "Some people if they buy you a beer, sooner or later they want sex or something like that. Not me. You do things for people because you want to, because you have a heart. That's me, it's the way I think."

One of the people here at Pauline's today is Leo. He and Pauline have known each other since they were kids. He's fifty. He sits quietly until prodded by the others, then speaks in a low, even voice. "For me it started when I was seven. My mother and father were working, so my brother would baby-sit. He and his friends liked to play strip poker. They raped me, starting when I was seven. After a while I started to like it. That continued for ten years, until I ran away." He was sixteen. "I never got along with my brothers, and I was fed up, I wanted something else." I'm curious for more detail. But I recognize in Leo's delivery a kind of cryptic short-hand; it strikes me as a way of managing pain.

From his mid-teens he became a regular at the local bars. "They were rough in those days. I never hid anything, and if they knew you were gay they'd pick on you; first thing you knew you'd end up with a broken leg or a broken arm. I don't know how many times I had to go to the hospital. Even if I walked uptown I'd get beaten up, right on the street, and nobody ever did nothing about it. I fought back, as much as I could." Why did he keep going back to the bar? "I was just stubborn I guess. I wanted to be there, and I wasn't going to change, no matter what they did to me. If I kept coming back, sooner or later they'd have to get used to it. And they did."

At sixteen he hitchhiked to Toronto. There he survived by stripping and prostitution, in the bars and on the street. "It was a hard life, but I enjoyed it." After several years he was diagnosed with muscular dystrophy, and spent the next ten years in and out of hospital.

Then he came back to Timmins. Why? "Well," he says, "it's my home. I'm close, very close to my mother. She and I take trips; we enjoy travelling together."

His four brothers, all miners, still don't speak to him. "I live alone, and mostly I stay by myself. Or I'll go visiting with friends. It's nice. I enjoy it."

The others at Pauline's place wait for more; so do I. But it seems Leo is done. Then he adds, "For young people today, it's so much easier, coming out. You can't imagine."

▶ 37 MY BEST FRIEND

HIGH ON A PLATEAU IN CENTRAL BRITISH COLUMBIA, "Eric Tor" built a nest for himself. The two-storey wood house overlooks a wetland, a blending of pond and swamp that curls away into the trees. A pair of shimmery wood ducks slide behind a grassy hummock. On the bank, a green canoe is parked.

Eric was born in 1952, in Vancouver, "to an ordinary family," he says, "where the father worked hard, drank hard, and beat the wife and kids." The eldest of four, Eric was the favoured target. "He managed to convince me I was entirely without merit or ability, and that all I deserved from life was hard work and misery." When he was ten the family moved to central B.C. In the small school there, a teacher noticed that the new boy, lonely and silent, had a talent for drawing. "That was probably the first time anyone ever affirmed me like that. Suddenly it occurred to me that perhaps I could actually *learn*, and from then on I wanted to learn *everything*."

At university, Eric found himself a girlfriend. "The fact that she needed me was probably the thing that I needed most in her." He insisted that the relationship be platonic. "Really I talked myself out of having to be sexual." The relationship didn't last, and Eric headed east to university in New Brunswick. "I had the ludicrous idea that I could go where no one knew me, invent myself all over again and start fresh."

In one of his science courses he found a friend, another budding naturalist. "Almost immediately I became absolutely obsessed with Steven; I made his life so miserable with my demands, he began to develop ulcers." Steven was heterosexual. "We'd arranged to share a house, but he decided – very wisely – to back out of it. That was the darkest time of my life." He swallowed a bottle of sleeping pills, but woke up the next afternoon. "At that point I realized that, like it or not, I would have to do something with my life."

Along with Steven and a young woman friend, Eric had discovered a passion for lichen, an enormously varied family of fungi that produce and live off algae, growing on rocks and trees like land-based coral. When a Finnish authority on lichen heard that Eric had been collecting specimens in a B.C. wilderness park, he invited him to Helsinki, and introduced him to the world of lichenology. Eric and his two university friends now rank as Canada's foremost younger lichenologists.

Studying in Vancouver, he waded gingerly into the urban gay scene. "I felt lost, a complete misfit." In 1982, now thirty, he decided to live where his passion lay. In a job teaching foresters about plants, he got to tour most of the province. Finally on the south edge of Wells Gray Provincial Park Eric found his place, in a magical blend of highland forest and meadow. From his front door he can paddle for miles into the bush.

We drive up into the park, then walk through the woods, emerging suddenly at the edge of an abyss. An immense column of water spews from a cut in the cliff, Helmcken Falls, at 465 feet the fourth highest in Canada. Mist born of the torrent drifts down the ravine. We sit as close to the precipice as my queasy innards will allow. Eric spots several white-throated swifts, first identified in this area by him. True to their name, they're fabulous aerial acrobats, even mating in mid-air. Then like a proud parent he shows me several varieties of lichen. Eric is quite clearly in love with his valley. Here he's no longer a misfit.

With pond and house under construction, he got a contract to work in Ottawa. "I decided that was it, I had to come out. Over the four months I was there, I must have slept with four men!" He fell ill, couldn't get a diagnosis, and became convinced he had terminal cancer. "It seemed so unfair – here I was finally starting to get comfortable with myself as a gay man, to actually feel desirable – and now I was going to die." The illness was eventually diagnosed as Epstein-Barr. He's still recovering.

In 1987, aged thirty-six, he moved into the partly finished house with a new friend, a fifty-six-year-old widow he'd met the year before. "It seemed unlikely I'd ever meet a man, and at that point I still couldn't face being alone." In 1992 she left, and tried to sell the place from under him. They worked out a legal settlement by which he would buy out her share over the next few years.

"It's as if my last crutch had fallen away. I was alone now, in this very isolated place, with no one to talk to, no one to touch. I just wandered around crying and feeling like squirrel dung. All the stuff my father instilled in me came pouring out, about my being worthless, unlovable and so on – I couldn't push it away any longer, it had to be faced. Through all that pain, I've found inner reserves I would never have guessed I had. Instead of being my own worst enemy, I started to become my best friend."

Hiking, canoeing, or skiing, Eric is within reach of woods, wetlands, waterfalls, mountain meadows ablaze with spring flowers, cariboo, curly-horned mountain sheep, and glaciers. At breakfast we have blueberries he picked last summer on a higher plateau – forty pounds of them in an afternoon. He gives courses and publishes extensive material on lichen, mushrooms, other flora and fauna of the area, and natural history. As it is everywhere, this corner of paradise is under seige. Eric has been actively involved in the campaign to preserve the park. The hostility this has sparked makes him quite guarded about being out. "I don't want to give them any more ammunition to silence or discredit me."

It's a chilly spring night. He stokes the fire. "Well, the nest is made," says Eric. "Now all it needs is for the right person to happen along." But how? There's not a lot of traffic up this way. Eric's friends – mostly straight, and tending to be in the arts – have standing orders to keep their eyes open. He's advertised in several rural gay publications and networks, continuously refining his message. A few of the men whose responses he liked have even made it here for a visit. But so far, the right person hasn't appeared.

What exactly is he looking for? "Well, it's certainly not just a penis. Of course I'm not opposed to sex – it would be wonderful if that worked out – but what I really want is a partner. Or an assistant – there's no shortage of work to be done around here. Either way, it has to be someone who's committed to a quiet rural life, and a life of ideas. Someone who can get as excited as I am about things like white-throated swifts. Someone who knows pain, and who's found in himself the wherewithal to deal with it."

He laughs. "I wonder – does such a person even exist?"

▶ 38 ONE OF THESE DAYS

DIANNE: "IT'S THE DAILY THINGS YOU MISS – THE chance to talk, a laugh, a reassuring touch."

Wendy: "There are so many good reasons for us to be living together. But what can we do?"

Dianne Crowell is forty. She lives on the south shore of Nova Scotia, in her grandmother's renovated barn, on land her family's owned for five generations. "That's my immediate blood family," she says, "as distinct from my extended lesbian family, which is much more widely scattered."

Two hours' drive up the coast, Wendy lives in a small house near the village of Cherry Hill. It's an old house that has been extensively renovated – after several years of debilitating illness, and nearly two dozen doctors, she was finally diagnosed with environmental hypersensitivity. Both her diet and surroundings have to be carefully controlled.

In her teens Dianne couldn't wait to get away from Yarmouth, "It had to be the redneck capital of the world." At high school she dated one of her teachers. Also the basketball coach; he asked her to drive some of the women's team to away games. "Of course it wasn't proper for me to stay with him, so I happened to room with this gorgeous player; she was six feet tall. The first time we kissed – this is God's truth – the bed collapsed."

She went away to university, came back to teach school, acquired a roommate, a woman. A little nervously, they became lovers. "Oh my God," Dianne recalls thinking, "It's that lesbian thing again." She was also involved with a man. "I'd always been attracted to all kinds of women for all kinds of reasons, but I also had good sex with men. There just wasn't the emotional connection; that only happened with women." She and her girlfriend caught the train west, and landed in Vancouver. She was twenty-four.

Some years later, with Dianne happily immersed in the lesbian community of Vancouver, her father suddenly fell ill. He asked her to come home and help out for a while with the family business. In fact the company was close to bankrupt. "I know eel fishing, I was raised around it, so I agreed to come back for six months. That was eleven years ago."

Since Dianne took over R Crowell Eel Processor Ltd & Smokery, the only such plant in Nova Scotia, it's grown from a regional to an international operation. From her upstairs office she negotiates purchases and sales of eels from along the Nova Scotia coast and mackerel from Newfoundland, to be shipped live on ice or smoked, primarily to Europe and Asia.

The sleek silver eel migrates from the Sargasso Sea in the south Atlantic, to mature in rivers and lakes along the Nova Scotia coast. They're caught at night, in weirs built into the rivers. Aside from the ones trapped in the Argyle River behind the plant, Dianne collects the catch in person, by truck, from the rest of the province. Some of the eels and all of the Newfoundland mackerel will be smoked in the adjoining smoke-house, one of her additions. She gives us a hunk of spiced, smoked mackerel. "It's one-eighth the cost of smoked salmon," she says. And very tasty – solid, tender, and richly flavoured in its lemon-pepper marinade.

Recently Dianne was appointed to the provincial Advisory Council on the Status of Women, as an open lesbian. After the story appeared in the local paper, she noticed a distinct chill at both her bank and insurance office. "I can deal with that. As a woman in the fish business, I'm used to having men turn their back on me while I'm speaking to them – or they'll tell me they want to talk to my boss. Let's face it, we're dealing with centuries of brainwashing here."

Growing up in suburban Halifax, Wendy did what the other girls did, she dated boys. "Some of them were great buddies, but I never experienced the kind of deep emotional attachment I was looking for." At twenty-one she went to work in a facility for female young offenders, "juvenile delinquents" in those days. She became close friends with a co-worker, and "it just naturally evolved into a sexual relationship. In the school environment this kind of open, comfortable intimacy wasn't considered abnormal." The two of them were partners for the next ten years.

Wendy is forty-five. As a parole officer with Corrections Canada, she monitors people on parole, works with sex offenders and perpetrators of family violence, and trains others to recognize and, if possible, to prevent such crimes. At the same time, as a volunteer with the local transition house she works with the other side of abuse, the survivors. "That's how I balance myself, by working with women, and the women's community."

I ask her if it's hard to work with men who hurt women. She hesitates, then replies, "The more I work with men, and see the effects of the violence *they've* undergone, the more I see that they need to be treated with a feminist approach – in this case a fundamental relearning of what's required to be a man. I know some feminists think you shouldn't spend much time on men, but if we don't, we'll just have to keep dealing with the consequences."

What does she say to the get-tough-on-crime fans? "Right-wingers really seem to like the bottom line. It's an absolute fact that incarceration costs a lot more than treatment – particularly if you add in the secondary costs to the family, welfare, the court system, and so on – and in the long run it's far less effective anyway. So there it is – the bottom line."

To a visiting friend, one of Wendy's male neighbours commented, "You'll never see a man over there. She has parties, and no men come to those either." "But the thing is," says Wendy, "it wasn't nasty, the way he said it. I haven't heard anyone say anything nasty. When I need something done around here, I make a point of hiring the worst reprobates in the area. If I didn't do that, those guys would be first out to scare the local lesbian. But this way they get to see that I'm a reasonable, decent human being, and now they'd protect me, no matter what."

Wendy and Dianne met six years ago, became friends and then lovers. When Dianne won the 1993 Woman Entrepreneur of the Atlantic Provinces Award, Wendy was her date at the formal awards dinner. Says Dianne, "She was absolutely stunning in her tux!" Aside from the other demands of a relationship, theirs requires considerable planning – and driving. "We hardly ever get to the city any more," says Wendy. "With our schedules it's just too complicated. That's hard; it tears you away from the culture, the new things that are coming in." They see each other as often as they can, and their phone bills are enormous.

In the summer a cycle of events keeps them in contact with their lesbian family. Wendy: "I have so little time to socialize, I want to do it with people who make me feel totally comfortable. That means women." There are weekend campouts at Wendy's and at a friend's lakeside cottage, murder mystery weekends at another friend's place, dances at nearby Broad Cove. "We just book the hall and get a DJ," says Wendy. "We've never had a problem. Last campout some guys came by in a pick-up and yelled a bit, but that's nothing to worry about." For Dianne's birthday next weekend, a gang of friends will go out for a cruise on a rented sailboat.

Living apart so much, is monogamy an issue for the two of them? Wendy: "We have always said that either of us is free to have other lovers, and we wouldn't fall apart if one of us strayed. But we've never actually tested that, and I'm not real clear how it would play itself out in real life. My last partner and I had an open relationship, and it didn't work at all. You can talk all you like about how you'd deal with jealousy and so on, but if it really came down to it, how well would we actually manage? I don't know. It would be a test, that's for sure."

Dianne: "I'd love to live with her. We're always scheming, trying to figure out how we could manage it."

Wendy: "Our schedules are out of control, it's ridiculous. But one of these days...."

▶ 39 A REALLY NICE BUM

"The hydro didn't get here til I was six. I remember what a thrill it was; me and my brothers would run home from school – a mile and a half – and fight over who'd be the one to switch on the electric light. I was ten before the phones came in. When we went from our one-room schoolhouse to the new school in town, the woman principal had to show us how to use the urinal."

"Ed" is a stocky forty-four, with hair and beard turning silver. He lives beside a swift-flowing river in north-central British Columbia, in a house he built, with neither electricity nor running water. Last year he finally put in a phone. He was born here, near a village that's not much more than a post office, a church, and the gas station where the Greyhound stops. A nurse, he works at a seniors' lodge in a bigger town down the highway. Except for a couple of brief spells away, he's lived here all his years.

"From very young I was always the oddball among my brothers. My dad wouldn't take me logging. I had no aptitude for it, whereas the others seemed to be born knowing what to do. He always said I was useless. I didn't like my father at all. He never knew who I was, and nor did he care." Until he suffered a massive stroke, and lived out his last seventeen years in a wheelchair. "He became much more approachable then, more emotional. By the time he died I'd actually grown quite fond of him."

From puberty on, Ed knew he was fascinated by men but sought out relationships with women. "Even though the sex wasn't any good, I'd still feel for a while that I really was a *man*. Of course that feeling never lasted, and neither did the relationships." When he was nineteen an older male cousin came out to him, and suggested they have sex. "I was terrified. I told one of my brothers, and he was really angry. He said it was my fault, I wouldn't attract people like that if I didn't wear my clothes so tight!" Twelve years later, at thirty-two, Ed would have his first homosexual experience with this same cousin and his lover.

We're sitting in Ed's living room, on an old brocade settee. The room is softly lit by oil lamps, their warm glow illuminating the dark polished dining room table, the china-cabinet, and the upright piano. He collects oil lamps; he has close to fifty.

Before he died the father portioned out land to the sons, giving Ed fifteen acres by the river. Ed built his house almost entirely by himself, in his spare time, learning carpentry as he went. "The first winter was so cold, I'd put the potatoes and onions in my bed so they wouldn't freeze." Forty below isn't uncommon around here.

In summer, like the sorcerer's apprentice he hauls his water in buckets from the river, boiling it to drink. In winter he melts snow on the wood cookstove. He bathes outside when temperature and the hungry bugs permit, otherwise in the kitchen. The outhouse serves year-round. Ed sews, knits, cooks, plays piano, guitar, and organ. He's gradually working up a vegetable and flower garden in the sandy soil. Bears often wander through, but usually don't stay too long. "I see myself preserving a way of life here that's just about gone. Sometimes though, I wonder just who or what I'm preserving it *for*. I guess it's a matter of pride; I want to show that it can still be done – or rather that *I* can do it."

He hasn't come out to anyone in his immediate family. "They don't ask, and I feel no obligation to tell them. I'm sure my brothers would fear that if I were out, *they* would lose status." And he hasn't told anyone at work. "I get more affection from my work family than my real one, and I'd be terrified to lose that." Most of the friends he grew up with have married. His best friend now is a married woman. "Her husband will make passes at me whenever he's drunk. One time he said, 'So when are you going to give me a blowjob?' I just told him, 'As soon as I catch my breath after the one you've given me.'"

The prevailing attitude to gay people around here is not promising. "I have a piano student, an older man, who says fags should all be taken out and shot." Ed's only two gay friends, a couple in the town where he works, have received threatening phone calls, and rarely go out. Now and then he'll drive an hour and a half to a gay and lesbian dance in Prince George. "But if you don't belong to one of the cliques there, you just don't belong – at least that's my experience. Even so, I'll go again. It's about the only place where I can be myself for a while."

As other men did on my travels, Ed asks me to keep my eyes open for possible mates. What is he looking for? "Well, I'm not as horny as I used to be. Now I'd want sex to be the icing on the cake." So what's the cake? "A man I can respect, and who respects me – in my family, nothing I say ever matters. I want his eyes to light up when he sees me. And it would help if he had a really nice bum. I've always liked a nice bum. I'd be perfectly happy just stroking it, for hours and hours."

▶ 40 THE NORTHERN MYSTIQUE

HEATHER DRIVES ME OUT TO THE HOUSE IN A MOTOR-boat. Last night we couldn't have made it, a heavy wind blew huge icefloes in off Great Slave Lake, clogging the bay – but this morning, they sailed out again. It's the end of May. Across the bay sits Yellow-knife. We tie up to the wooden deck, constructed on a series of huge steel flotation tanks. This is the houseboat that Anne and Heather built, two storeys tall, spacious, airy, and colourful inside. It hardly rocks at all. The "honeybucket" sits discreetly to one side, awaiting tomorrow's regular collection.

Anne Lynagh is thirty-two. She grew up in Zambia, where her father was a Roman Catholic teacher, and then in Lethbridge, Alberta. "As a kid I was pretty asexual. I knew I didn't particularly want the kind of male attention that rates the size of your tits, but then I didn't really have any alternative either."

She dated boys, longed to touch her best girlfriend in the youth group Katimavik, and at twenty she was kissed for the first time by a woman. Here was the alternative. "After that I was right in there, full speed ahead." She worked awhile in Edmonton, but got fed up with her job. "I also figured I must've slept with all the women in the city by then," she laughs, "and since I had a friend up here, I thought I might as well try it out." Almost immediately she got work with a local film company. She's also the only female technician at the local CBC station.

Now thirty-three, Heather Haye grew up on a farm in south-west Ontario. Through her early teens she was disturbed by the crushes she had on other girls, but once she'd found some material on homosexuality in the public library, "Suddenly I realized this was me, I was one of *those*." On a ladies night at the gay bar in nearby London she met her first lover, "a recruiter of baby dykes." Then she fell in love with a woman who turned out to be a junkie and ended up in the hospital from an overdose. Heather headed north, to Yellowknife. "It was about as far away as I could get. I lied my way into various jobs, and in no time I was thoroughly hooked on the northern mystique." Now she works as a computer consultant.

"What I wanted more than anything," says Anne, "was to live on a houseboat. So I just started working on it." For a bottle of scotch a local engineer helped plan the base, built on forty-foot-long sealed tubes. A lesbian architect designed the living space. Curious about the massive anchors being built out of snowplow blades down at the docks, Heather started hanging around. Anne: "Most people just wanted to chat, but she was prepared to do some actual work." Anne had a girlfriend at the time, but she had no interest in the project. Heather: "By the time winter was coming in and ice was starting to form on the bay, most of the other volunteers had got jobs or it was too cold for them, so finally it was just the two of us, hanging from a rope, nailing shingles up on the roof."

Anne: "The more time we spent together, of course the more we talked." Heather: "Eventually we got into deep stuff, the real life questions, like how did Anne feel about her current relationship? I didn't want to play around on her girlfriend, and neither did she. Also I want kids, so we talked a lot about that." Anne: "I'd never left anyone for someone else, so I wanted to be sure that if I did do it, it was because I wanted out of that particular relationship, and not just for greener grass."

One night Heather heard from a friend in town that Anne was free. "There was a huge blizzard that night, but I walked out to the houseboat anyway – I got there about three AM." Anne: "The ice was still weak; she could easily have fallen through. And there was nothing here, just a mattress and a sleeping bag." Heather: "We sat up and talked the rest of the night." Anne: "I'll tell you, if you want to meet a partner, there's no better way than building a houseboat."

A major challenge of living on a houseboat is getting to work every day. Heather: "After a while you learn to read the ice, how it forms in horizontal plates or vertical candles. Of course it can happen that you misread it." When the water is open they travel by boat. Later while the ice is forming they walk across, dragging a canoe. When the ice gets strong enough they use a skidoo, getting up enough speed to skip over wet or weak sections. Finally in the dead of winter the ice will support their ancient car.

Before heading back in the boat, I want to check on the baby project. Heather: "There's no sperm bank here, so if you took that route you'd have to fly out, which could get impossibly expensive. Besides, I'm not too interested in the father being an anonymous little packet of sperm. I want the child to know him. I've spoken to a few men about it, but most of them are married, and their wives aren't too keen. Personally, I'm tending to favour the turkey baster routine. I think that would do the trick quite nicely, thank you."

▶ 41 MANLY THINGS

A YOUNG GUY IN A PICK-UP WANTS TO BUY A NEW RIFLE. David Cole compares prices and features for him on two models. Behind the counter, self-help books are lined up neatly on a couple of shelves – David also runs a mail-order book service. By the lunch counter hangs a row of moody landscape photographs, mounted, priced, and signed "Robert Lincoln Hebert." Out back it's feeding time for the young trout. David's assistant tosses a pot of food into the tank, the water boils, it's a feeding frenzy – young trout have the table manners of piranha.

David Patrick Cole – aka Robert Lincoln Hebert – is thirty-nine. He lives by Picture Province Pond, in Kings County, New Brunswick. According to local maps the forty-acre spring-fed pond was dug 150 years ago. David has turned it into a U-fish operation, with fish supplied by the aquaculture project he's developing. He buys trout eggs, hatches them in a climate-controlled room built onto the gunshop, then raises them to fingerlings in the tank. As soon as they're big enough to fend for themselves, they're released into the pond.

David was an only child. From about age three, he went hunting and fishing with his father. At six he fired his first rifle. One day in the woods, a teen-age David asked his father if he ever masturbated. "Never," came the reply. "I want to talk about sex," said David. Without looking at him, his father said, "There's only one person in our house who's doing any dinging, and that's me. Now this conversation is over." David recalls, "I won't say he aimed his rifle at me, but I clearly remember he swung it in my direction and I ducked. I was scared shitless; I wanted to vaporize. That was the end of my sex talk with my dad."

Though his sexual fantasies were exclusively male, David continued to believe for many years that he must be heterosexual. Of homosexuals all he'd heard from his father was that they were fairies who flitted from tree to tree. "I did all these manly things – hunting, fishing, cutting wood – how could I be gay?"

Out hunting, David and his father had come across the pond. "This place ever comes up for sale," said his father, "you buy it." Shortly after his father died, it did, and he did. By his early thirties he'd moved here. The first year was rough. "I had no money, and the paperwork for welfare was so humiliating I told them to keep it. If I hadn't been able to hunt, I would've starved."

One night he became so agitated he couldn't sleep. "All these childhood memories suddenly started welling up, some of them pretty ugly. That went on all night, and by the end of it I was quite suicidal. But then I heard a voice, this child's voice that I'd completely forgotten about. He said, 'Look, it's not done yet, we've got places to go.' That's the voice I've been following ever since. It's led me to places I didn't particularly want to go, but by then I didn't feel I had much choice." For example? "Well, for one thing I didn't *want* to be gay – given prevailing attitudes who would? I had tremendous fears about coming out in such a male environment. How were people going to accept a homosexual gunsmith?"

Outside the small lodge that David built for himself and guests, we sit on a couple of shiny old car seats, on the deck overlooking the pond. Brandy, a big, comfortable dog, snoozes at our feet. It's a warm day in early October; the pond is ringed by flaming trees. By the far side of the pond, a solitary fisher trolls from a rowboat. Ospreys, cormorants, herons, and kingfishers all compete for the catch here.

David saw a therapist for a while, and began to come out to people he knew, one by one. "I lost a few – who knows, maybe their own sexuality was threatened – but fewer than I'd feared. Some even thanked me; they said I'd given them the chance to know me better. I think heterosexuals need to know us; it's a great loss to them if they don't." When he came out to his mother, a very conservative Catholic – "a religious addict," he calls her – she erupted into a lengthy sermon on sin.

At this point, so far as he knew David still hadn't met an actual gay person. He heard of AIDS Saint John, the closest thing he could find to a gay organization within reach. He called to offer his services as a volunteer – but hung up when someone answered. "I was really torn, I guess, between my lingering homophobia and thinking, well, how am I ever going to meet anyone if I stayed holed up here all my life." He called back, made contact, and was introduced to Freeman Patterson, a well-known landscape photographer who lives halfway between David's place and Saint John to the south.

"Freeman was the first gay person I'd ever met. And I believe he was also the first person to be genuinely concerned with my soul. When I took one of his photography courses, he took me aside and said, 'David, I want you to take the chance to be you.' That was really scary for me." With his first camera when he was ten, David snapped clouds, snow drifts, and telephone poles. His father told him if he couldn't take proper photos – people, cars, and houses – he didn't deserve to have a camera. "When I came back to the workshop with the photos I'd taken – *my* photos, close-ups of rust patterns in an old washing machine drum – the other people stood and clapped. Nothing like that ever happened to me before."

Why does he sign his photos Robert Lincoln Hebert? "That was my original name – I was adopted. The name is all I have left from that life, so why not use it? I guess it has something to do with recovering that lost, innocent child, which is what I hope to do in my photography." He's tried to trace his birth parents, but so far he's been blocked by both the Roman Catholic Church and the provincial government.

Last year David placed a want ad in the Halifax-based *Gaezette*. Of the replies he got, only one touched him. The man came up to live here for a season. But he wasn't happy so far removed from an urban life-style, and left. "I'd love to be with someone," says David, "and I'd love to be a parent – at least I know a few things *not* to do – but I wouldn't do it alone. It's hard enough to get it right with two of you! But while I used to feel I *needed* a mate for my life to be complete, these past few years I'm getting much more comfortable just being with myself. I've found a new friend, someone I hadn't really ever known before. And he's not a bad sort of fellow, not bad at all."

▶ 42 OFF THE GRID

THE LITTLE BOAT STRAINS, ITS OUTBOARD MOTOR groaning against the tidal current that surges through the narrow gorge. Salt spray stings our faces. It's a heavy load, seven of us: Robin and Alice, two lesbian friends of theirs from another island, Brian, me, and T'lou, a grey bear of a dog. This end of Cortes Island has no roads; boat is the only way in.

Over the motor and the rushing tide, Robyn yells, "You have to learn how the wind and the tide interact – if you get flipped round broadside to the waves, you've had it." Alice: "One time in a bad south-easter I got thrown overboard. If I hadn't been wearing a survival suit...." She shrugs. Robyn: "Some days we don't dare go out at all; we just stay home until the storm passes." It's a joy to reach their sheltered floating dock. The house is built high on the rocks, but when an incoming tide conspires with a winter storm from the southeast, twenty-foot waves will coat it in icy, salt-laced spray.

Robyn is forty; Alice, a year older. On a British Columbia holiday in her early twenties, Alice had fallen in love with the coastal encounter of mountain and sea. She moved west from Ontario, lived in various places along the coast, then returned east. Robyn visited the province as a tree planter, also in her early twenties. It was clear to her this was where she wanted to be. She returned home to Toronto to complete her master's degree in fine arts, then worked as a graphic designer. One day on the Toronto island ferry she spotted Alice. They both lived on the island, but hadn't met. Says Robyn, "She kept saying 'we' this, 'we' that, so I assumed she must be with a man. It turned out the other part of the 'we' was her dog, Pax." Alice: "He was right there beside me; you'd think she would've caught on." Old Pax died a few days before we arrived here, and grief is still in the air.

Alice and Robin became lovers. Master's degree in hand, Robyn took off by motorcycle for a holiday in the Yukon. In the meantime Alice had inherited and sold her grandmother's house in Toronto. She headed west again, and Robyn south, to seek their dream place between the mountains and the sea. Finally they found it – a drafty, ant-eaten cottage and cabin on a rocky point of Cortes Island, between Vancouver Island and the mainland.

At age twelve, Robyn had "my very first lesbian affair. It was cuddly and snuggly, and my parents were openly encouraging us. They were quite puritanical and terrified of sex, but apparently they saw what we were doing as quite innocent, and not sexual at all. Little did they know, and nor did I." By her early twenties she had a male lover whom she intended to marry. "Then I went into primal therapy. It was wonderful – suddenly I remembered who I was, a lesbian!"

"I also had a little affair when I was twelve," says Alice, "but then nothing, so I just figured I must be straight – until I was majorly seduced. Robyn and I were actually seduced by the same woman." Robyn: "We've talked about starting a newsletter for all the women who've been seduced and dumped by this woman."

It's early May. Darkness is gathering at the huge south- facing windows. T'lou has settled for the night, out on the deck. We've just finished supper, plump oysters we collected off the rocky beach just before the tide came in, and simmered on the wood-burning cook-stove. Alice and Robyn live off the grid, beyond reach of the hydro. Their refrigerator, water pump and heater, computer, and radio-phone are all solar-powered, from the big rack of photovoltaic panels out front. A tower and wind-generator are on the way, to be trucked to the island and then hauled out to their place in sections by boat. Wind power will fill in when the sun isn't available.

With help from a couple of Alice's exes on the island (both genders), the two of them rebuilt the house and cabin, learning as they went. It took a year, full time. A composting toilet converts human waste into soil. Water pumped from two shallow wells is stored in tanks behind and above the cabin, for delivery by gravity flow to bathroom and kitchen taps in the house. "My best skill is research," says Alice. "All these systems are pretty site specific, so you have to be very clear about what it is you're trying to do."

The cabin at the other end of the cove serves as a studio and guest house. Robyn: "When you're together as much as we are, it helps to have a place where one of you can escape. I need to get off Cortes more than Alice does. I need contact with other people in my particular communities, especially the arts." She's just back from a lesbian gathering on another island, "nothing to it, just four ferries away. It was wonderful to be steeped in that culture again. We were drumming and singing, dancing, story-telling, art-making. I'd almost forgotten how much I need that kind of contact." And Alice? "This is home for me. There's no place else I'd rather be." Robyn: "Barnacles leave Cortes more frequently than Alice does."

They make their livings as they can. Alice: "I work mainly with people on social assistance. There isn't a lot of existing work here; you have to create your own, and most people have to do three or four different things to get by. So we're trying to get folks on assistance to look at what skills they have, and to stretch a little, to get beyond the fear that there's nothing they can do."

Robyn, a graphic designer, works on environmental projects, most recently a sustainable living guide for newcomers to the island. "Either it'll scare them off or give them some useful information." From atop the steep, rocky hill behind their house, plumes of smoke from Campbell River's pulp mill are visible. "The chlorine in the mill effluent is killing the oyster beds around here, among other things, so we launched a campaign to promote the use of chlorine-free unbleached paper – now it's gone international."

Reflected sun plays on high cliffs across the water. Out of sight up there, ghostly figures roam across the rock – animals, hunters, gods perhaps. These are petroglyphs, rock paintings, the imprint of earlier inhabitants. Like most Canadians, Alice Grange and Robyn Budd live on Indian land. Unlike most Canadians, they are planning to give it back. This is a sacred place. The new owners discovered that, long before the European invasion, a village nestled here in the shelter of the hill. Many villagers died of smallpox, from infected blankets given them by missionaries. Alice: "Aside from the obvious issue of justice, I also have a lot of discomfort with the whole idea of private land ownership. So we've been having discussions with native chiefs and elders to work out some kind of land trust agreement by which the land can be returned to them after we die."

Early morning. High, feather-brush clouds. A dozen eagles spiral up there, halfway to heaven. In the dark Pacific water, silver flashes – tiny fish. A seal surfaces with hardly a ripple, peers at us a long moment, then snorts and dives. The only sound now is breath, wind in the ancient pines.

V

The homosexual agenda

▶ **43 HOW IT IS**

THE HOMOSEXUAL AGENDA? AS FAR AS I CAN TELL IT'S
to live a life worth living. We're strange that way.

This book is about people I happened to connect with along the
way. This chapter is about the ones I didn't get to meet.

I was struck continuously by how many of us have contem-
plated or attempted suicide, to exit a life that others had made intolerable. Imagine then how many of us have succeeded at it. A U.S.
government study that was suppressed by the Bush administration
found that one in three teenage suicide attempts is directly related to
struggles with sexual orientation. It can't be much different here in
Canada. So many life stories, harshly cut off, are missing here.

The people in this book are survivors. I was surprised at how
many of us are in recovery from alcohol and drug addictions. I didn't
select people for this aspect of their stories. In a way they represent

all of us, first in their overwhelming drive to numb the pain, then in the even stronger yearning to be free. Absent are people who haven't yet found their way out of this particular jungle. Their stories wait to be told.

I met some remarkable rural gay men who are living with HIV or AIDS. But a great many more are missing here. So many have died, or fled to the city. In the Northwest Territories I heard repeatedly that the virus had virtually emptied Yellowknife of a thriving gay male community. They went south in search of more sophisticated health care, or to die in more familiar surroundings. I heard of a gay couple who left Toronto to live in the New Brunswick village where one of them grew up. When word got around that he was HIV-positive, they were run out of town, back to the anonymous safety of downtown Toronto. He's dead now, that much sooner perhaps due to the ignorance of his neighbours.

Nor did I get to meet the people who'd been run out of town simply for daring to express who they were. In Pictou County, Nova Scotia, two lesbians I met used to know a gay man whose house on the main street was frequented by local young men seeking sexual favours. Everyone knew, but a delicate conspiracy of silence prevailed. Then he became lovers with a black man, and in so doing broke an unwritten law. When he refused a blowjob to one of his regulars, the man threatened to kill him. The two gay men left town. Several years later the white one came back, married to a woman. He'd learned his lesson.

Many people never heard of my search, and many others weren't interested. There were some, however, who were both aware and interested, but still we never met. One gay man in Alberta sent me a hand-written account of his sex life, in almost clinical detail from puberty to the present, but concluded his letter by saying it would be too dangerous for us to meet. That's the word he used, dangerous. This from a province where members of the government speak openly of shutting down their human rights commission – they say it's wasteful and unnecessary.

From an older (than me) gay man in northern Saskatchewan, I heard that several of his friends had turned down my request to meet.

My assurances of confidentiality made no difference. When I pressed him for reasons, he told me they feared if they allowed me any access at all to their lives, I might use it for extortion. This was the clearest expression I heard of the suffocating fear in which so many of us still live.

I didn't get to meet some lesbians because I'm a man. Of these, some would only share their stories with another lesbian, and some not at all. Recently a friend of mine, an urban lesbian, met some of these very private women in a small Ontario town. She reports that they live quite discretely, do not refer to themselves as lesbians, and bridle at any mention of feminism. Their social lives revolve exclusively around other self-supporting women who also live in couples. They are intensely uncomfortable, she says, with anyone who's single, and even more so with anyone who's out.

At the Canadian Tire store in a northern Ontario town, my host points at one of the cashiers. "She's that way inclined," he says, in a private undertone for public places. "How do you know?" I ask. "Everyone knows. Her lover teaches at the high school; they've been together thirty-six years." "But how do you know all this?" "It's a small town; you just know. She and I have never spoken about it; of course we never would. But she's always been especially nice to me."

Everyone knows. No one's talking. We do what we have to. And for many of us, that's just how it is.

▶ 44 FLOWERS IN THE DIRT

HE SHOWS UP AN HOUR LATE AT JIM SAVILLE'S SPRING Valley Ranch in southwest Saskatchewan.* The forty-kilometre drive through the Cypress Hills wasn't the problem; he's used to that, in all weathers. His tires were flat, and the battery drained nearly dead by the lights being on – they've done it again. "I don't bother to lock it," he says. "They'd only break a window."

---

* More on him in Ch 18

When we negotiate names and anonymity, he insists I use his whole name, David Stewart. "It's a matter of principle. And what could happen that hasn't already?" This is a brave man. He's thirty-four, works in the tourism office up on the highway, lives in a small apartment behind the store on main street in Maple Creek. Along the narrow walkway to his door, David has planted a row of hardy prairie flowers in the dirt.

His family's been ranching here since ranching began. He remembers being asked in grade four to report what he did on the ranch. "I didn't know what to say. What you do on the farm is what defines you as a male, but my father never took me out to show me any of that. It made me feel there was something horribly wrong with me – the only conclusion I could draw was that he didn't like me."

About age five he recalls watching TV one afternoon with his mother. "Suddenly there on the screen two men kissed. My mother was horrified, she said, 'That's disgusting, those men are sick!' I can remember very clearly, I ran into the bathroom and threw up. Until recently I'd always assumed my reaction was the same as hers, disgust at two men kissing. Now I can see that I was actually reacting to my own excitement, and my mother telling me *I* was disgusting, sick, and therefore unlovable."

David grew up in exile. "From very young I felt I didn't belong in my family, I wasn't worthy of them. So many aspects of me simply shut down. It's hard to find words for it – I didn't know what I was feeling, if anything – I guess I was pretty well numb. I didn't have any friends. I read a lot. As for being gay, all I picked up was that gay men were depraved and frightening – and I would have done anything to avoid being like that."

By his late twenties he'd become executive assistant to a cabinet minister in the former Conservative government of Saskatchewan, notorious for its rabid public stands against homosexuals. David drank heavily, and developed eating disorders. "You wouldn't have liked me in those days; I was one sick boy." Then he fell in love, with a man. The relationship collapsed, and David ended up suicidal. "I was lucky to find a psychiatrist who didn't judge me. I think that was the first time in my life I ever felt safe."

He came back to Maple Creek to heal. It's a cowboy town – dusty streets under a big sky, pick-up trucks, pointy boots, big hair, line-dancing at the bar. "At least every other day someone hollers 'faggot' at me. When I cross the street I've had trucks race at me. I've had vandalism to the car, and to the house. One Christmas Eve someone tapped at my kitchen window. I looked out and saw a guy with his pants undone; he was masturbating and motioning with his finger for me to come out. He'd also look over his shoulder as if he wasn't alone. I'm sure it was a set-up; they were trying to lure me out there. I was terrified. The phone was within reach, but I was too scared even to grab it and call the police."

What does he do with all these insults and assaults? "Sometimes when I'm hollered at I'll go home and cry. Sometimes I avoid the street – it's really humiliating to be yelled at like that. But other times it doesn't bother me so much. I feel we have a responsibility to be who we are, to be out there for the sake of gay youth, so they won't be so messed up as I was."

A local group formed to grapple with the problem of teen suicide, rampant in the area. The chairperson is a fundamentalist preacher. When he wrote in the Maple Creek paper that homosexuals are barred from heaven, David decided to attend the next meeting. "I've seen statistics to the effect that thirty percent of teen suicides are gay, and I couldn't allow that not to be raised. It was very scary to go in there, and I was made to feel quite unwelcome, but I did present my information. This is my community too, and my young people who are dying." Next day on the street a rancher thanked him. And two local ministers asked him for more information. "I've also proposed to the vice-principal at the school that they organize some kind of support for gay and lesbian kids. He seemed quite receptive."

What keeps this quiet hero in Maple Creek? Is there anything here for him? "I see a man in Medicine Hat, that's not too far. He's also a ranch boy from the hills, and he's helped me to come out. It's not a very intimate relationship, but he's someone to share the night with once in a while." And there's Jim Saville here at the ranch. The two of them are easy and warm with each other, kidding and affirming in the same breath. "You can't be gay, you dress funny." "*I* dress funny? Where did you get that belt, Canadian Tire?" David came to Jim's annual gay weekend last August. "It was wonderful to see so many of us together like that, outside, free – it made me feel so good I cried."

Any day now, Maple Creek will be losing David Stewart. "I don't believe there's much more I can do here in the way of healing. I'm just about ready to move on, to get out there and start building my life again in the larger world."

Someone else will have to tend those flowers in the dirt.

▶ 45 GOD'S COUNTRY

IN THE EDMONTON BUS TERMINAL I BUY MY TICKET TO a small town about two hours east. The ticket agent says, "Hey, I grew up there. That's God's country." Oh-oh. I've heard that Aryan Nation organizers do well out this way. A few weeks ago an anti-gun control rally filled a stadium here. When the local Reform MP suggested meekly that it mightn't hurt to put some...er, um, well, slight controls, you know, just on the automatic assault weapons, he was loudly booed.

The bus drops me at a convenience store. The town has one street about a mile wide, two churches, and two grain elevators. A steady stream of pick-ups and big old cars turn in diagonal to the curb. Each driver checks me out as they go into the store. I squirm. Where the hell is "Raymond"? He suggested we meet here in this anonymous town. A canopy of dark clouds fills the sky, torn by white light at the horizon. Dear God, could this be the wrong town? But here he is, in a fire-red Chevy Blazer. We barrel up a dusty side road, and I breathe again. He parks between the road and the ditch, among fields of young grain that carry on in every direction to the far horizon. It's early June.

"When I was a little kid," he says in a mellow baritone, "I guess I did a bit of hero worship on the parish priest. I liked him, and I wanted to be like him. Looking back, I recall that he was incredibly handsome." Here were the twin pulses that would drive Raymond's life. He's forty-two, a Roman Catholic priest, a chaplain on an armed forces base in northeast Alberta, and gay.

In his teens he had a girlfriend. "But there were always these furtive glances at men, in changing rooms and places like that." He had his first sex with a man at nineteen, and at twenty his first relationship, lasting five years. The other man wanted to settle down, but Raymond didn't. Fresh out of university he entered the seminary in Toronto. After two years he was clinically depressed, and went to work for a computer company. In his second relationship he wanted to settle down, but the other man didn't. By 1982 the impulse to priesthood had returned, so he went in for post-graduate theology in Ottawa. "I was determined not to fall in love again, but in my second year I did. He rebuffed me, and I pulled back, way back. I was really angry and bitter about it." In 1986 he was ordained a Roman Catholic priest, and took vows of celibacy. "I meant to keep them, I really did."

Three years later Father Raymond got involved with a man. "It didn't develop into anything, but it certainly did reawaken all the feelings that I'd repressed." By now he'd joined the military, as a chaplain. On his days off he'd go into the city, to meet other gay people. Sometimes in the bars he'd recognize priests. He chuckles. "Some of them when they saw me, they'd be out of there like a bat out of hell!" Now he's in a relationship again, with Henry in Edmonton. "The Pope may not like it, but everyone needs someone to love; it's only human."

Raymond lives off the base, in town. "A rectory is a fishbowl; if you fart everyone knows about it in twenty minutes. In town there's a little less scrutiny." This is the Bible Belt, not famous for tolerance. "Sometimes I overhear conversations on the base or in town that give me the shivers – ferocious, vicious gay jokes, or I'll hear people say they'd beat the shit out of them; there's even talk of mutilation. I'll gently question their Christian commitment, and wonder aloud if gays and lesbians can really be the demons they make them out to be. Some listen, others won't. I just keep at it."

He also cooks once a week at an AIDS hospice in Edmonton. "I've lost friends to the disease, and I've seen people shunned and cast out for it. No one should have to die like that – if I ever got that sick, I'd certainly hope there'd be someone there for me."

Despite the positive 1993 Supreme Court ruling on gays in the military, it's still not the most hospitable place to be lesbian or gay. "Now and then people do come out to me. A chaplain is usually considered to be a pretty safe bet – it's confidential and we're supposed to be non-judgemental. One person told me they were under suspicion and they were being harassed. Under the circumstances, I suggested they think seriously about whether civilian life mightn't be a healthier place to be."

In 1992 the Vatican ordered U.S. Catholic bishops to campaign actively against any gay civil rights initiatives that came up on state or federal ballots. "I'm tired of the Church telling me I'm intrinsically disordered or evil. I'm neither. And when the Church says it's okay to discriminate, I can't accept that." Father Raymond argued thus in a letter to *Xtra!*, the Toronto gay and lesbian paper. A month later, his command chaplain confronted him with the letter. "He asked me if I was gay. I'd already said so in the letter. 'Are you sexually active?' 'Sometimes,' I said, 'but don't worry, I'm discrete.' He told me if I didn't stop, there could be repercussions – it was a threat. And this guy is as gay as a Christmas tree! But he's also very career conscious. I don't understand how these people live with themselves."

Father Raymond fell silent – for a year. Then he saw a letter in *Xtra!* from a fundamentalist preacher, listing all the biblical reasons why homosexuals are consigned to hell. "It really annoys me when people abuse the scriptures like that. We can hurl bits of scripture back and forth at each other all we like, but why not take the example of Christ himself, and actually *live* the word of scripture for a change, which is about love, not hate. That's what I said in my letter."

Why does he hang on in such a medieval institution as the

Church of Rome? "Well, believe it or not the Church has always been a source of comfort for me. Even when we disagree, it's still my family, my community – or one of my communities. Despite everything that's been done to us, there are still significant numbers of us gays and lesbians in the Church, and we have all kinds of gifts to offer. They can't keep turning their backs on us. The Church has to change, that's all."

Last I heard, the Vatican isn't famous for being open to change. "True enough. And the day may come when I have to leave, as so many others have done. But I won't do it voluntarily; they'll have to throw me out. As long as I can, I'll carry on, I'll be a thorn in their side. I'm Irish, you see, and very, very stubborn."

46 THE WEB OF LIFE

BECAUSE HE PROTECTS THE SHEEP FROM WOLVES, THE donkey is named Super Barrio, after the Mexican comic character who fights for the rights of the poor. One of the dogs is Eduardo Galeano, after the Uruguayan freedom-writer. The milk cows are all named after heroines – anarchist Emma Goldman, Guatemalan activist Rigoberta Menchú, Jane Rule*, and such. On this farm the animals are neither commodities nor accessories; they're characters in the drama of life.

Each of the mailboxes along the country roads in Pictou County, Nova Scotia, bears a single name, a man's name – the wives are assumed. At this farm the box has two names, spelled right out, Jane Morrigan and Catherine Hughes. When Brian and I arrive, the morning chores are done and the afternoon ones not yet begun.

Instead of naming the farm or the herd after herself, Jane did the opposite: she changed her birth name to that of the farm's original owners, Morrigan. Forty-four now, she grew up in a Montréal suburb. Since she finished high school at seventeen she's worked in

---

* More on her in Ch 33

farming, first with horses, at a posh resort in Jamaica, then for a wealthy family in New York state. Where did this impulse originate? "In my head. I grew up in an atmosphere of so much distrust and suspicion, where any desire for independence was seen as selfish, and creativity as foolish. I saw my father humiliate my mother so often with his authoritarian stuff; he'd reduce her to tears. And I was suffocating – not as a lesbian then, but as a young person – I wanted to get the hell out of there."

At twenty-one Jane married a man. Two years later at agricultural college she fell in love with a woman. In 1977 the two of them drove across Canada looking for a place to farm, and settled finally on a rented farm in Pictou County – the other woman and her two kids, Jane and her two horses. Jane got work as an artificial inseminator. They took a loan and bought the present place. A couple of years later the partnership ended, and the other woman departed with her kids.

Through the mid-'80s Jane maintained her job, worked the farm herself, and had relationships of varying intensity with a variety of people, both women and men. Along the way she ran into trouble with other lesbians in the area, a fragile community at the best of times. "Through all those years I was quite fearful of losing my job – this is a very conservative area – and I stayed in the closet. I had in mind that I'd give it ten years, so people around here could get to know me. All in all I was painfully isolated." Eventually she reached the point of contemplating suicide.

"What got me through that time were two things. One was my farming community – straight people. When I injured my back they sent in meals, and every day for six weeks a straight couple came in after they'd done their own chores to do mine. I didn't have to ask, and they wouldn't take any money. The other thing was my connection with animals and nature – the animals' non-judgemental love, and my awe at the beauty of this land, the seasons, the whole web of life." Then in 1986, nine years after she arrived in Pictou County, Jane met Catherine.

Catherine Hughes is thirty. She grew up in Kingston, Ontario, with a two year sojourn in Kenya. Her parents are South African expatriates, her father a university professor, her mother a professional potter. "At home there was always lots of discussion about the big issues – socialism, communism, feminism, apartheid – and lots of encouragement to be myself, to think for myself." But for Catherine there were limits. "In high school I had crushes on girlfriends, and I did know some lesbians, but I never said a word or did anything about it. In fact I dated the brother of this one woman I was very attracted to."

At art college in Halifax, Catherine came out. In 1986 she went with her lover, Anne, to a summer weekend for women in Pictou County. There they met Jane. The three of them became friends. Catherine and Jane fell in love. Catherine and Anne returned to Ontario, where Catherine joined a women's construction brigade bound for war-torn Nicaragua. When she got back, she finished art college in Halifax, commuted back and forth to Jane's farm, and eventually moved in. "The relationship, this place, working on the farm – all of that has really inspired my artwork."

An example of Catherine's art: a pavilion of bent saplings is covered in felt, made from the fleece of the farm's own sheep. On the inside walls are painted images, tree roots and a bird, vibrantly coloured but trapped below ground. Inside the pavilion lesbian voices tell their stories, gathered on audio-tape by Catherine. "It's a relatively safe space in which we can share our stories," says the artist, who is present when the work is shown. "Relatively" is the key word – when the pavilion was installed at a new gallery in Pictou, the nearest town, Catherine asked one of her parents to be present, to diffuse – well, whatever might happen. "In fact it went really well. Because we'd taken a risk – Jane too, by association – and the work was obviously from the heart, people were quite receptive. Some of them even got talking about their own stories, which was great."

In the living room hangs a wall-sized multimedia work, *Seeds of Change*, an homage to the Mexican artist and communist Frida Kahlo. "It's about the generative powers inherent in the natural world, but also the power of ideas and art to counter various forms of oppression." In Pictou County, oppression assumed a very vocal form in the outbursts of the local federal MP, Roseanne Skoke. A right-wing Catholic, she has called homosexuality immoral, unnatural, and a threat to the family, and linked it to pedophilia and bestiality. Ironically, new legislation on hate-based crimes from her own governing Liberal party provoked some of Skoke's most virulent attacks.

On the first day of October 1994, some 150 people gathered on the street outside her constituency office in New Glasgow. It was an unprecedented show of community strength by lesbians, gay men, bisexuals, relatives, and supporters, some with placards declaring themselves "Straight But Not Narrow." Catherine and Jane helped organize it. Jane: "I've been involved in other issues like the Gulf War and Oka, but Skoke's remarks made it very clear to me that some energy had to be shifted into defending my own group. Given the tendency of human history to repeat itself, I have no doubt that the rise of the right wing is a very serious threat."

Across the street a crowd of hecklers tried to shout down the speakers and singers at the rally. Jane: "Some of them were actually screaming at us, 'fuckin' dyke,' 'dirty faggot,' and so on – it was frightening to see that degree of hatred so boldy expressed right out there in the daylight. On the other hand I think it may have given some of the bystanders a little taste of what we're up against – you know, the kind of comfortable liberals who wonder why we make such a fuss?" When we came through Pictou County, Jane, Catherine, and others were making plans for a public forum on homophobia and human rights, a speakers bureau, and a workshop for local schools. Pictou County will never be the same.

Meanwhile back at the farm, it's early November, overcast and quite cool, seven AM – milking time. Two cows are milked at a time, by machine, the milk carried through overhead pipes to a refrigerated holding tank, awaiting transport to the dairy. Cleaning one of the cow's teats, Catherine leans her head into Emma Goldman's broad brown side, and talks quietly to her. Her hands are red from the damp chill. And life goes on....

ON THE SAME SUMMER DAY WHEN NATIONAL TV NET-
works ogle bums, breasts, leather, and drag at the huge Toronto pride
parade, fifty-three gay men and lesbians gather on a grassy slope in
eastern Ontario. They eat, drink, camp, swim, cruise, gab, dance, and
generally let their hair down, until the mosquitoes drive them
indoors. Out here among the woods and stony eruptions of the
Canadian Shield, this event seems a bit improbable. A few years ago it
would have been impossible.

The catalysts are two city boys who turned off the fast lane
eight years ago, onto a back road north of Bancroft, where they
remade an old farm house into a guest house called Wildewood. A
portrait of its patron saint, Oscar, greets you at the door, as does Bru,
a pony-sized Newfoundland dog. Your hosts, Joey Shulman and Barry
Siegrist, are both forty-five. They met fifteen years ago in Toronto.

An army kid, Barry grew up on the move across Canada, but as
far back as he can remember he's always wanted to live in the country.
He'd already managed it once, with a lover who later died of AIDS.
Joey was born in Newfoundland. "I think I must be the only Jewish
fag that Newfoundland ever produced." For years he too dreamed of
"a little white house with nice flowers and a picket fence – it was a
Beatrix Potter sort of country fantasy." "In fact," says Barry, "getting
Joey to leave the city was like pulling teeth."

A self-confessed type-A personality, Joey pursued his Toronto
arts promotion career with ferocious energy. Another opening,
another show defined their lives, always on the go. Barry: "We could-
n't have kept up that pace much longer; we were burning ourselves
out, fast." Joey was offered a job as director of communications at the
Centre for the Arts in Banff, Alberta. "It was perfect," he says, "that
idyllic, incestuous little place in the mountains."

Three years later, in 1987, Joey tested positive for HIV.

Barry: "We knew so little about it back then. Did he have a
month to live, a year? So we made an instant decision to fulfill this
long-standing dream of moving to the country." Joey: "Both of us

suddenly felt a really strong need for home, a secure, safe place."
They headed back east, a U-haul trailer in tow. Finally on a roller-
coaster road through the woods, they found a hundred acres with a
run-down farm house, and set about realizing their dream. The renovation and landscaping took a year, and cost a small fortune. It
includes an Olympic-sized pond.

"We'd always lived as if the money would never run out," says
Joey. "Now here I was on a disability pension, and the end of that was
in sight." "And it was pretty clear there weren't any jobs we could do
around here," Barry adds. Hence the guest house – not only does it
provide income, but it keeps them in touch with the gay world outside. The day I arrived there were two other guests, lesbians from
Tennessee and Trinidad.

For many of us with rural fantasies, a common deterrent is the
fear of being all alone out there in heteroland. Barry nods. "Oh yes,
we imagined all kinds of things – burning crosses on the lawn and so
on." Joey adds, "We had one couple to dinner from the town who said
they'd been told if they sat on our sofa they'd catch AIDS." A six-foot-
high wooden fence along the road discourages the idly inquisitive.

Every person I interviewed in this area, lesbian or gay, was suggested by Joey. Several told me they'd never known another gay person around here until Joey and Barry arrived and started making connections. All this in eight years; how did they do it? "Well," asks Joey,
"where do you look first for gays? In the arts, of course." They joined
the theatre guild in Bancroft, thirty minutes drive to the south. Joey
laughs. "Twenty-five percent gay – it never fails!" Want ads in *Xtra!*
brought in a little business, a threesome or two, and a couple of good
friends. Beyond that, says Joey, "You just keep your eyes open, you ask
a lot of questions, and you stay as out as you dare." Active in the local
business association, he played Santa Claus in one of the Christmas
parades. He laughs. "I wore my yarmulke under the Santa hat, just in
case. But I really do think involvement like this buys us respect – at
least they can see we're benefitting, not harming, the community."

Joey gets massage from a therapist in Bancroft, a lesbian. With
her partner she runs a guest house for women, and the two of them

know dozens of other lesbians in the area. The two couples negotiated an unprecedented New Year's Eve party, with men and women together. People who'd passed each other on the street for years, and wondered, now met face to face. And so community grows.

Joey is working in their open kitchen, starting on supper – roast chicken, brussels sprouts, squash, crab and avocado salad. What about the HIV? What role does it play in their lives? Joey: "If we'd continued to live the way we did in the city, I'd be dead by now for sure. Our lives are simpler here, and much more physical. Unbelievably physical. And for nine years now I've been well, really well." He knocks on the wooden cutting board. Barry: "We still hesitate to make any long-range plans. We've done a lot of renovating here really fast. Now we're sort of coasting." Joey: "Catching our breath."

After quitting one doctor who turned out to be anti-gay, Joey found another who's willing to work with him through the many complex health challenges that can arise from HIV infection. "Having worked in a hospital, I know it's not where I want to end up. But if I were sick and at home, it could get to be quite a burden for Barry. We'll just have to face these things as they come up."

Joey rolls out dough for an apple pie, tonight's dessert. "You know what I think is the real challenge for us out here? We don't have any map to follow. No one's been this way before us; there are no tracks. We really have to find our own way. We're pioneers."

▶ 48 CHAPTER EIGHT

"I WAS VERY METHODICAL ABOUT IT. I GAVE NOTICE ON my apartment, sold everything I owned, rented a car and drove to this park with a beautiful view of the city. I hitched up the vacuum cleaner hose I'd bought, one end to the tailpipe, the other into the car, taped up the window, turned on the ignition, and waited. I'd imagined you just went to sleep. After about twenty minutes I was choking and gasping for air, I was turning *green*. But I kept thinking I have to finish this, I have to die. Eventually I couldn't stand it anymore; I threw the door open and fell out onto the ground. Then I had to take the car back."

It's a warm, cloudless June afternoon. The rye-bronze fields hum with cicadas. "Nick" is showing me his adopted town, population 650 or so, two hours by bus from Winnipeg, Manitoba. The ballpark, the hotel, the laundromat. "One time in January I was doing my laundry, and this guy kept looking at me – you know, in that gay way – so we got talking, about wood heat. I invited him over to look at my woodstove. Well, what was I going to say; I don't have any etchings. But he said he had to get home, he was from the next town. I haven't seen him since."

This could be called the seventh chapter of Nick's life. He's forty-six. In the first chapter he's born in the port city of Saint John, New Brunswick. He vividly recalls admiring the bum of a schoolmate in grade one. Summers he helped out at his uncle's dairy farm. "I didn't think much of the work, but I did love the solitude; I'd walk for hours by myself through the fields."

By grade seven he had a boyfriend. "The two of us had a really active sex life, and no inhibitions at all. We carried on with just about any guy that was interested, the scout master, sailors off the ships – we had a wonderful time."

In chapter two, Family Values rears its ugly head. The two boys were separated by their families. "I still carried on with men, but I started to feel guilty about it, dirty somehow. Basically I wanted to hide, to become as hetero as possible." He dated women, and married. Nick wanted to see what lay beyond Saint John, so he and his wife moved to Vancouver. Within two years they both realized the marriage was pointless, but remained friends.

Chapter three. "It took me awhile to get back to feeling okay about being gay. I joined a couple of gay groups, got a little bit radical, but mostly bounced around the bars in Vancouver and Toronto." In his teens Nick started doing drugs. By his late twenties in Toronto he was addicted to speed. After drying out in the slower confines of Saint John, he returned to Vancouver.

Chapter four, the high life. "A series of jobs, essentially frivolous but sufficient to support a nice apartment, a nice car, a couple of relationships, a fair amount of travel, lots of partying, and *lots* of sex." He details some of the latter, not bragging so much as fleshing out the picture. I'm astounded – the *stamina* it must have taken!

Chapter five. "By 1986 I was seriously strung out on coke, totally consumed by it, and I'd started to free-base crack. Everyone I knew was an addict too; it was a whole gay subculture. Any friends I'd had earlier had dropped me by then; they were fed up. I saw other people lose everything for the sake of the drugs, and I was getting deeper and deeper in debt. So I got out." Back to Saint John. "But after a year and a half I'd had it. From where I'd been, I found gay life much too narrow and restricted there." He headed west again, stopping off to visit a friend in Winnipeg.

Chapter six, 1988. In Winnipeg, Nick was diagnosed HIV-positive. He signed up for an experimental drug study taking ribavirin. It made him sick. His doctor urged him to continue for the sake of the study. "How was I to know; maybe some good might come of it, maybe I could contribute something." He got sicker, became anemic, couldn't sleep, lost thirty pounds. "Finally I said 'fuck it'; I flushed the drugs down the toilet, quit the study and the doctor." Immediately he began to recover.

Another doctor recommended AZT. "On paper it sounded okay, so I took it. Exactly the same thing happened, all over again." His doctor suggested lowering the dose, but the patient wanted out. "I found that even going to the clinic got really depressing; it was all about being sick. And no one would listen to anything I had to say." He quit the drugs and the clinic. "By then I was in kind of a meltdown; I just wanted it all to end." He did his best with the vacuum cleaner hose. Then he found a counsellor who listened. After trying another little town, he settled here. Far from the fast lane, it's not even on the highway.

Chapter seven, the present. He lives in a tiny house with a huge backyard, on long-term disability topped up by a small monthly allowance from his father. He gets occasional odd jobs at $6 an hour, and the rest is barter – he'll clean a couple of carpets for a load of firewood, or drive an elderly woman for the use of her car two days a week. "Believe me, that helps when it's thirty-five below and windy, and you *have* to go to the laundromat because you're out of clothes." Anything extra – a new chimney last year – has to be done on credit. His landlady is decent, but not interested in spending any money on the place. In winter winds, the curtains on the window shiver.

A couple of married men from up the road will drop by now and then for a beer. One of them turns up while I'm there – black t-shirt, tattoos on a beefy forearm. Conversation turns on how to locate studs in the wall, for an electrical outlet Nick wants to install in his kitchen. After "Ed" leaves – "The wife'll be on my back" – Nick says, "I enjoy the contact, up to a point. But there are so many things you can't get into, and they are *so* serious – talking about studs there I had to bite my tongue not to make jokes." Me too. Once in a while his gay friend will visit from Winnipeg. "And that's about it for my social life, gay or otherwise."

He hasn't seen a doctor in two years. "And I've never felt stronger. Last winter I split seven truck-loads of wood, no problem. One of these days I'll stop smoking. And at some point I guess I ought to re-connect with a doctor, in case something happens."

Is he content? "Once in a while I miss holding a beautiful man in my arms. Most likely he'd be HIV-positive too, and in a similar financial situation – two of us could afford to buy this house and fix it up; we could even put on a second storey."

For now, Nick's garden sustains him. He gives me a tour, in loving detail. Until last year the apricot tree bore less than a handful of fruit. Then he pollinated it. As if blessing the tree, he waved a branch of blossoms cut from a neighbour's tree over each of its lower limbs, and then tossed the blossoms high into the parts he couldn't reach. This year the tree is loaded with little green apricots. "My neighbour says they make quite a good wine. I'll have to find out how to do that."

Chapter eight.

IT'S LATE MARCH, COLD AIR, WARM SUN. SNOW STILL huddles in the shadows. In the comfortable twilight of the barn, sheep and chickens clamour for attention. Piers Gilson introduces me to a set of four-week-old lamb triplets, adorable, out of a fairy tale. Their mother bawls at us. "You haven't made yourself sick again, have you?" Piers inquires crisply, the starched head nurse. "She was quite sick for a while; we had to bottle feed the triplets." As we turn to leave the barn, the din escalates. "They're very social," says Piers. "They do not like to be left alone."

Piers and his partner, Sandra, are both fifty-two. They operate two farms, 900 acres in all, in the rocky, wooded hills near Algonquin Park in eastern Ontario. Living in the house they built, they raise sheep, selling rams for breeding, lambs for meat, and the fleece for wool. "I can't imagine not having animals around. But now with my health slipping, and Sandra's chronic bad back, we've had to cut down – we used to have close to two hundred sheep." To make ends meet they also sell electric fencing and outdoor wood furnaces.

Born in England – the accent is still there – Piers has never thought of himself as anything other than gay. "I was sexually active from about fifteen, and for some reason never had to go through the agonies that others have suffered. When I told my mother, she said she'd known for years. She's expressed concern at some of my choices of boyfriends, but what mother doesn't?" For many years he lived in Toronto, working in theatre as a free-lance stage manager and technical director.

Twenty years ago two friends, a heterosexual couple, bought a farm up here. The man was killed in a fire that levelled the original farm house. Sandra decided to stay on and asked Piers to help her rebuild, between theatre jobs. "I came up, and we've been cohabitating ever since. Our relationship is very close, equivalent in many ways to a marriage, but not sexual. Perhaps that's why we've managed to live together so long." A quick laugh. Both talk and laughter tumble out of him at speed, as if trying to catch up to his thoughts.

"I've had my boyfriends up here, introduced them to anyone who came by, we've been to social functions together – and of course word gets around, people figure things out for themselves." Though city dwellers often regard country folk as rednecks, Piers says, "People here tend to be individualists, and quite tolerant of eccentricity. As long as you fit in certain ways – not coming on with an attitude of superiority, being reasonable with your neighbours, helping out when needed – it's not really that hard to be accepted."

For almost a decade Piers has assumed the thankless job of township fence viewer and livestock evaluator, with the authority to settle fence disputes between neighbours, and to assess compensation for farmers whose animals have been killed by predators. These two functions bring him in contact with many people, and once word got around that his decisions were careful and fair, the contacts became increasingly comfortable. "I'm sure I have more friends than I ever did in the city. If we need something heavy done, we can easily get twenty people together for that. If a house burns, you'd be amazed how quickly a new one can go up – people take care of each other here."

In 1987 Piers found out he was HIV-positive. His approach to treatment is primarily to prevent the infections that can do such damage to an already weakened body. He relies on conventional medications, but also investigates alternatives like Chinese herbs. "Conventional medicine tends to deal mainly with symptoms – the idea being to keep you comfortable until you die – whereas a more holistic approach looks at causes too, and perhaps even longer term solutions."

Many people with HIV assume that access to sophisticated – read urban – medical services is essential. Piers' experience differs. With no T cells left to protect him, so far he's managed to avoid any serious infection. "I'm so rarely in crowded places – subways, bars and such – and hardly ever in high-stress situations. In fact if you look at the statistics, we're actually tending to get longer survival figures in some of the rural areas than in the cities where all the big hospitals are." This shift wouldn't have happened without rural activists like

Piers. "The way I look at it, you can die from AIDS or you can live with HIV. I don't see how you can live with it unless you're honest about it, and being honest about it means being out. I'm quite sure that more people are dying of shame and fear than from the disease itself. If you're ashamed to tell anyone you have something that's in your very cells, how can you hope to be well? How can you get the services and support you need if you're in hiding?"

Piers' creed is simple: "I don't want anything more than anyone else, but I will take nothing less." When a doctor at a local hospital hesitated to touch him, he refused any further medical treatment or advice from the man. He's given interviews on living with HIV to the local paper and TV station. With another gay man he founded the AIDS Committee of North Bay and Area, and now he works on the board, also with the provincial AIDS network. "It's really important that people with HIV be involved in these organizations so other board members can't get away with lumping us into a blanket 'them' – we have to keep reminding them, 'Hey, that's me you're talking about, I'm a person and I'm still here.'" The AIDS Committee functions include locating supportive doctors, lobbying for medical and social services, safer sex education, and the forming of support groups for people with HIV.

Has his high public profile cost him? "On the contrary. When I've let people know I'm HIV-positive, they're really concerned. I'm gradually losing muscle strength, which can be damn frustrating on a farm, so I'm asking people for help more often than I ever used to. They'll say sure, and they don't expect to be paid for it. It's almost as if you're giving *them* a gift, the opportunity to participate in your care."

Farm work is exceptionally demanding; so is the HIV battle. "I tire easily these days, so I have to be careful how I use my energy. I have to meter it and use it where it's most needed. I've got a modem; that helps me stay connected with less travel. But the discipline of having to get up in the morning, having to go out and tend to the animals regardless of the weather – it's these things that keep me going. I don't envy people who've been forced to retire, I really don't. Not for one second."

"I'M A WOMAN OF THE PRAIRIE," SAYS "ELENA." SHE'S forty-five. "I grew up on a farm in the '50s, in a community very much like this one. And I spent a lot of my childhood trying to get out – rural Saskatchewan was too small; I craved something larger." The prairie, too small? From their garden you can see to infinity in any direction. "I don't mean the land and the sky – there was no end to that – but the options, the openings seemed so limited, so narrow. From a very early age I knew I was different, and what I longed for was a larger world where I could test out some things, with fewer eyes to watch and to judge." She did get away, for twenty years, but now she's back. "I still have a love-hate relationship with this place. Right now, in the spring, I love it."

"Right from the beginning," says "Madeleine," "I despised the prairie. I came here from the west coast with my husband, to a small-town church in the early '80s. Those were drought years; everything was brown, and windswept, and bleak. There was no shelter any-where. But after about five years I began to notice that somehow this landscape had actually begun to inhabit me. Now I think it's become my way of seeing the world, my interior landscape." Madeleine is forty-three.

Their landscape starts from a compact, warmly renovated, cen-tury-old house, and a garden the two of them have made – grass, hardy flowers, sprouting vegetables, a few slender trees. Beyond the fence, a scattering of modest houses – no more than thirty people still hang on here – and the classic prairie silhouette, a grain elevator, no longer in use. Beyond that is land and sky, the only boundary between them a wall of darkening cloud, pierced now and then by lightning. A fierce wind comes up, lashes the trees. Rain hits, sheets of it. Hail rat-tles and thuds on the roof. Then as quickly, the storm passes.

The first time Elena came across the word "lesbian" in an ency-clopedia, "I was jubilant and horrified, both at the same time." She was fifteen. She dated boys "for cover." She was leaning toward min-istry in the church she'd grown up in, the Lutheran. "I wanted so much to be a nice girl. I was the oldest daughter, for God's sake, I was always looking for people to help – so I found the perfect place to do that."

In the early '70s, as a lay minister in northwest Ontario, she immersed herself in the struggle for native rights. "It was hard work, but a hell of a lot easier than having to face my own issues." After the armed native occupation of a local park split the congregation, Elena was encouraged to leave. She went to seminary in Saskatoon, became increasingly politicized on women's issues, then on sexual orientation.

Along the way she'd been ordained a Lutheran pastor, and for years she led a double life. "In my first relationship, neither of us would even speak the word 'lesbian.' Talk about denial!" Then the Lutheran church enacted a policy that no self-declared lesbian or gay person would be ordained, and the few who already were ordained would be removed. "They were saying we couldn't be ministers if we dared to speak the truth about our lives. In other words we'd be tolerated as long as we agreed to remain dis-integrated. That *really* pissed me off." In 1990 Elena left the church to which she'd committed so much of her life, or as she puts it, "The church left me. I'm still working to get my life back, after losing it for so long to the trappings, the title, the demands of the church."

Madeleine grew up in rural Prince Edward Island. What was the source of her impulse to ministry? "Insanity," she says, with a laugh. "I used to work with kids who had cerebral palsy, and it maddened me to see how the medical system treated them as a bunch of malfunctioning parts. Right from childhood I've always identified most strongly with kids and old women – they have the deepest kind of wisdom, and they deserve a place. In those days I was still naive enough to believe the church was that place, where wholeness would be celebrated and everyone would belong."

After a tour of duty in the Roman Catholic Church, she went to theology school in Halifax. "I've never experienced so much sexual harassment in my life. I certainly wasn't a feminist yet, but I was starting to question things. I remember in one seminar a male student yelled at me, 'Shut your face, you catty bitch!' And the faculty did nothing. I thought, this can't be happening, this is the *church* – I really thought I was going crazy."

Becoming gradually more defiant, she held on. She was ordained to ministry in the United Church, went to Vancouver, and married. She and her husband came to minister in drought-ridden Saskatchewan. Then for several years Madeleine found work, and a home, at the Prairie Christian Training Centre in the Qu'Appelle Valley. "That was the first place I found where I could really express both my beliefs and the skills I was acquiring. It was grand."

And her sexual journey, how did that go? Madeleine takes a breath. She's seated in the corner of the sofa, her legs drawn up. "The only sexual identity, the only sense of body I ever had as a child was derived from abuse." She chooses her words with careful precision. "As I matured, the connection I developed with women was more of a kindredness than a sexual attraction. I think for me there was a real feeling of safety in being asexual. So my journey has meant coming to terms with myself both as a woman and as a sexual being. What I realized eventually was that I had neither the desire nor the energy to be with men."

In 1981 Madeleine and Elena met at a church conference. Both were still in relationships; their own began in struggle. Elena: "For me the most contentious issue was monogamy. As a feminist and as a les-bian, I really didn't want to be locked into the traditional nuclear cou-ple thing. But I found I just didn't have the capacity to maintain two intense relationships at once." Madeleine's marriage ended. "But I'd unlearned so well any sexual sense of self as a child, it was really hard for me to acknowledge my sexual attraction to Elena. For the first six months I was easily threatened and often quite angry. I felt like a fourteen year old with all this new learning to do. I still do, sometimes."

Most of us who were raised Christian learned that sex and the spirit are entirely separate; one's up there, the other down below. Elena shakes her head. "What a crime it is to teach people that. In fact being sexual – loving, being loved, sharing embodied pleasure – is *so* life-giving, and that to me is exactly what spirituality is about."

Madeleine adds, "So many of us learn that sexuality has nothing to do with pleasure; instead it's about abuse of one sort or another – and reproduction. To me it's a miraculous thing when people can get past those barriers to simply love each other in this very profound way. It really is; it's a miracle."

People without cars are stranded here. Regina isn't that far, but rural buses are all but extinct. So Madeleine, in joint ministry here with two other women, will often drive her elderly neighbours to the doctor. Elena commutes to the city, where she does adult education with seniors. Their house, rebuilt by and always lived in by lesbians, is known locally as "the girls' house." To more than one battered woman it's also become known as a safe house, a house free of men.

Elena serves on the town council, along with two men. "We make a contribution, and I think we're appreciated," she says. "We're gradually taking more chances, like showing more affection with each other outside, in the garden." "I agree that we're appreciated," says Madeleine, "but we're not really *known* here for who we are. It would be nice to have people of similar values nearby. As it is, if we want to stay connected we have to drive all over creation."

Through six months of brutal winter it's tempting to just stay home. "So we'll deliberately plan alternatives. Right now we're working on a women's trip to Mexico." Now and then they'll put on a women's dance at the local community hall. Elena: "We book the hall for a private party; people do it all the time for family functions." Madeleine: "We do have a couple of women designated as bouncers, just in case. But so far they haven't had anything to do."

And then there's "Hope." The fourth child of Elena's sister, "Beth," she was born with a high spinal cord injury, near total paralysis, and a complex array of other disabilities. Pain dominated the first year of her life. She couldn't swallow, had to be fed through a tube down her throat. "That was so hard to do," says Elena. "We were always scared of hurting her, and she hated it every time." At five months a tube was implanted in her stomach. Since then she's been living half the week with her birth parents and siblings, forty-five minutes' drive from here, and the rest with Elena and Madeleine.

"The nuclear family just couldn't hold up under the pressure," says Elena. "Even Beth sees that now; she says what kind of stupid invention is this anyway?" Madeleine adds, "It's become clear that the members of Hope's extended family who are in heterosexual relationships haven't been able or willing to offer nearly as much energy, time, and commitment as we have." Elena organizes her work week round Hope's schedule. "It's the first time I've ever done that, planned my life around family needs." Madeleine nods. "Last Friday, at one of *many* meetings we've been to, trying to educate the health system about people with disabilities, Beth introduced me as Hope's other mother. In a place where the long-standing pattern is possession – men possess the land, women possess the children – that was a pretty remarkable gesture."

When it's thirty below out there, when the wind won't let up and winter seems eternal, sometimes they dream of moving away. "But as long as this is where Hope is," says her other mother Elena, "this is where we belong."

VI

Over the rainbow, somewhere

▶ **51 AUTUMN, THE NINTH**

OUT THERE IT'S A JUNGLE, THE CORPORATION RULES.
But we've paid off the mortgage, the garden produces a little more
each year, and while I wrote this book, Brian was building us a real
Bathroom.

For eight years, in all weathers, we've made our daily pilgrimage
to the outhouse. Now we have a composting toilet. It doesn't compost
our effluent half as well as the outhouse did, but it is *indoors.* A city
friend mourned the loss of the outhouse: "It was so rustic, so *you.*" He
visited once in the winter, and never came back. Memo to rustic
romantics: the outhouse is still open for business.

For eight years we bathed standing up, in a plastic tub by the
kitchen sink. This arrangement had a certain pioneering virtue to it,
but it was so taxing to set up we'd often let bathing slide another day,
or two, or three.... Now we have Gigi in residence, a creamy six-foot

tub with a sloped back and molded arm rests. We didn't name Gigi; it's the model. We could have chosen a Delphine, or an Anna, or a Patricia – ladies, it seems, are meant to lounge about in scented bubbles while men shower the way they pee, upright, ready for action. We have this option now too, a real shower. Upright or not, if cleanliness really is next to godliness, then we must be approaching divinity.

As a project the bathroom moved from one-of-these-days to top priority about the time I started travelling for this book. Quite suddenly my hands were in serious trouble, some of the fingers painfully bent; I couldn't open jars; even turning the ignition key in the truck took both hands. Walking hurt. Sitting hurt. Frightened, I went to a rheumatologist. Peering over half-glasses, he examined most of my parts, making grim noises over his shoulder at the resident.

Finally he informed me I had "quite the case" of psoriatic arthritis, a condition in which for some mysterious reason an overactive immune system turns on its host, attacking the connective tissue. He advised an HIV test, and prescribed what he called "a nice little drug." *HIV*? "It can sometimes cause flare-ups like this." But I'd already told the resident that Brian and I had been monogamous for twelve years. "Still, wouldn't hurt to check it out." Why was I so afraid?

I happened to have done some advance reading. His nice little drug is a powerful cancer medication whose possible side effects include destruction of the liver. "We'd monitor you carefully," he said, a faint smile landing on his face like a butterfly in transit. I refused the drug. The smile flitted away. A difficult patient. "All right then, we'll try you on an anti-inflammatory," he said crisply, and vanished.

I was ice cold; my jaw clenched. My hands trembled so, I could hardly undo the hospital gown. I wanted to cry, but couldn't. I imagined telling Brian he better make the bathroom wheel-chair accessible. I imagined – well, you can imagine. Living here is physically challenging enough as it is, quite labour-intensive. Would it now become impossible?

The HIV test was negative. I cancelled my return appointment with the specialist, threw out his prescription form, and went to see a naturopath. She's more interested in health than disease. I've changed my diet, and take a variety of herbal and homeopathic supplements. Don't get me wrong, it is still with me. (I tend not to name it, at least not in the doctor's way, which doesn't seem helpful.) Mornings, my joints creak and grind like hinges unoiled for a century. I move more slowly now, with greater caution; for example, sex of the acrobatic, sweaty genre has receded to the realm of nostalgia. Pain of some degree is a constant companion, and fear of disability hovers often at the edge of my thoughts. But then life, after all, is a fearful occupation. On the other hand I can open most jars now, the ignition is a snap, and I hurt less after a walk than before. I still have my liver. And we have this divine bathroom.

I'm drowsing in the tub, gazing through curls of steam at the world darkening out there. Hundreds of crows whirl from tree to tree, talking all at once, a parliament of birds. An early snow has dusted the garden and woodpile. In four days of heavy work we felled and cut our whole winter's firewood. Once again our good neighbours, the two brothers from down the hill, helped us haul it up to the house with their ancient red tractor and home-made wagon. The logs are out there now in three long, tidy stacks, warming just to behold.

I sink deeper into Gigi's liquid embrace. After five decades of fighting the world's imperfections and my own, I ache. As a child I learned my lessons well. Long before I knew I was gay, I'd been taught that in some undefinable, fundamental way I was deeply flawed. No matter how hard I tried, I could never quite be worthy, not as a straight boy, not as a gay militant, not as writer, friend, or lover; never, never could I be good enough. If, as Susan Sontag says, illness is metaphor, then my metaphor is a life-force cruelly at odds with itself, a civil war within. I ache from the struggle, and I'm desperate for a truce. So I'm learning Tai Chi, to move through the world not with less power but perhaps with fewer collisions. And I'm learning to meditate. As I understand it, the goals are an ever-deepening, non-judging awareness of what is, balance, and gentle compassion, for self and others. Each of these strikes me as a novel and sensible idea, probably good for the world but definitely good for me. Now if I can only learn to stay awake when I sit to meditate....

But. There is always a but. Hannah Arendt wrote of the "inner emigration" practised by German intellectuals in the '30s. Those who couldn't or wouldn't leave the country escaped into their own fantasies, their version of Gigi's sheltering depths. These days the prospect of escape gets more and more beguiling. They are out there, the other side of the garden, just beyond the woods – don't you hear it, the faint but distinct thud of jackboots?

For most of us this is something new, something for which we can hardly be prepared. What do we do, arm ourselves? They always have a bigger gun. Turn out the lights then, and hope like hell they go on to the next house? They'll be back. Anyway, who can live like that, trembling forever in the dark?

I think of people I met in the course of writing this book. Ordinary folks like me. We won't make the national news, likely not even the local paper, probably not so much as a tiny item buried between the hockey and the weddings. But here we are, still kicking, still loving. Working things out with the neighbours. Returning a tentative smile on Main Street. Visiting the local MP, again, after he claims yet again that there are no homosexuals in his riding. Keeping on, as Heather Bishop says in one of her songs. Taking all kinds of crazy chances, doing what we can.

That's it then. That's what we do. And yes, dammit, it is good enough. It is.

▶ 52 I AM

ROBERT MICHAEL WORKS IN THE CONVENIENCE STORE on the Shubenacadie Micmac reserve in Nova Scotia. A middle-aged woman comes in to buy Kleenex and pop. A couple of boys hang around the counter. "One of them is gay," says Robert, after they leave. "He's only twelve, but he told me he was gay. He said, 'You're fighting for me too.' I know at least ten kids on the reserve who are gay."

Born in Boston, Robert moved here at six when his mother remarried. "I only found out he wasn't my real dad when I was twelve.

That kind of blew my mind." By eight he knew he liked boys. "When I was eleven or twelve I was supposed to go out with this girl, but I liked her brother better, so *we* went out instead. Lots of guys here will fool around as long as you don't say nothing."

When he was ten, in grade six, he got both ears pierced and went to school with two earrings. One ear was supposed to mean you were straight, the other gay. His friends asked what both meant. Definitely gay, said Robert. He was sent to the principal's office. The principal asked him to take off the earrings, they were disturbing the other students. The earrings multiplied, to four on one side, three on the other.

He's finished work now, and we're sitting in the kitchen at his parents' house – they're away – with his dog, Lucifer, flopped in the corner. At twelve Robert bleached his dark brown hair. His father demanded to know why he'd done it; was he a faggot? "I said 'Yeah, I am.' He beat me up, right here in this room. All my mother said was, 'Don't tell anybody.' The next day my father took me down to the drugstore, and dyed my hair brown again. I went to a friend's place; she got it back to white, and I put in green and blue. As soon as my dad saw it he grabbed me and pushed my head through the wall – right there." A calendar hangs where the hole used to be. "My dad's an RCMP officer. He and my mom both drank; they were selling drugs and fighting a lot. I'd often pretend I was sleeping so I didn't have to deal with them."

Robert wore fishnet nylons to school. He dyed his hair orange. He wore eyeliner. He shaved his eyebrows off. He wore t-shirts saying "I Can't Even Think Straight," and "Queer Nation." Didn't he feel a little, well, out there? "I didn't care what anyone said. I had no friends here on the reserve anyway; they wouldn't have anything to do with me." At fifteen he started going to the gay bar in Halifax, and at eighteen he took the train to Toronto. "I got in with this young punky group up there. Some of them were into leather, or they'd be drag queens, or transsexuals. I met thirteen year-old transvestites in Toronto."

Why did he come home? "I didn't fit. I didn't do drugs, and I wasn't white – some of them turned out to be skinheads, white supremacists. The only natives I saw were prostitutes, most of them on crack and living on the street. And I started to see people dying of AIDS – these good-looking, muscular guys, they went really fast. I started to think if I stayed there I'd end up dead." When he returned to the reserve he was nineteen. "This is where I belong. If anybody doesn't like it, too bad, here I am." How are things between him and his father? "After he got caught drinking on the job, he decided he'd better dry out. Things got better after that."

In 1992 Robert decided to run for election to the band council. "There's nothing here for young people – no jobs, no prospects, and we don't have any say in how things are run." In public his opponents called him "faggot," "child molester." Rumours were spread that he had AIDS. "I figured to hell with it, why even bother to campaign. Even so, I got eighteen votes." This year Robert and a few other young people on the reserve persuaded nineteen-year-old Allan Francis to enter the elections. Robert ran his campaign. Their experiment in democracy ended in eighty-six votes for Allan.*

These actions haven't won Robert any friends in high places. He's twenty-seven now. For several years he's applied to the band council for a place of his own. "My uncle is a band councillor, and he told me they brought my name up once, but they said because I was gay and wouldn't be having any children, why did I need a house? They said I might as well get off the reserve and move to the city. But I don't want to live in the city; I want to live here."

Whatever he does, Robert Michael is not going away. He's determined, and he's an optimist. "Things could be worse," he says in a deep, level voice. "When we're walking back from town, maybe nobody gives us a lift, but at least now they don't stop their cars and start fighting with us anymore. Like I said, things could be worse."

---

* Allan's story comes next.

▶ 53 DREAMS

ALLAN PUT ON THE DRESS HE'D CHOSEN, ONE OF HIS best, and applied his makeup with even more care than usual. Then he walked with his campaign manager to the all-candidates meeting. "I went in there and sat down. I looked very nice, and I was being the nicest person I could. But some of them started getting buzzed. This one guy came over to me and said, 'By the way, we don't need no fuckin' faggot in for council, and we don't need no fuckin' faggots on the reserve either.' Then he walked away. I thought, Oh my *God*! I was going to tell him off, but Rob said no, because of the election. We called the human rights commission but they weren't interested. So I sued him."

Allan Francis is twenty-one now. He receives us on a pull-out bed in Robert Michael's living room. The two of them have been friends since Allan was eight. Like a 1930s movie star he reclines in a shamble of covers, dimly lit by a splash of light from the kitchen. His dark brown hair is streaked with purple highlights. He yawns, stretches, a weary hand flutters to greet us. It's been a rough day, for a long time.

Allan was born here on the Micmac reserve near Shubenacadie. "Ever since I was little, everyone knew I was gay. When I'd walk down the hall at school, they'd jump me. I'd get in fights and I'd get thrown out. I went to a few schools; the same thing always happened. So I quit. And I'm not the only one, school didn't work out for lots of people around here – either they were sexually abused, or they're gay and they're trying to hide it. I never tried to hide a thing."

At fourteen he started to do drag. "It was the only way I could get into the bars [in Halifax], by pretending I was a woman. I'd use fake ID; it was never a problem. I've been dressing in drag on and off ever since. There's not a day you'll see me without makeup on the reserve. Sometimes I'll do the clothes too, and sometimes not. This is the way I am, and if they don't like it, too bad."

At fourteen he also came out at home. "There was this huge fight, so I hitchhiked to Ottawa and stayed with a friend for a month. When I came back it was the same old bullshit, so I took off again, to

Over the rainbow, somewhere – *175* –

Toronto. My father called me on the phone; he was crying, please come back. So I did. He said he didn't care if I was gay, he still loved me – that made me happy. He's dead now. My mother – well, she was pretty hard to get along with, him being an alcoholic and everything. But I was the one they all picked on; my brothers and sisters did it too. So I told my mother, either accept me or I'm out of here for good, you'll never see me again. We still yell at each other, but it's not so bad anymore. Sometimes she'll even buy a dress for me."

Allan gets mixed reviews from the community. "Half of them accept me and the other half don't at all. There's lots of them who are gay themselves, but they're scared shitless to come out. If you have sex with a guy here it has to be this big secret. They'll say, 'I've got a baby,' or something like that. Oh, *puh- leeze*." Allan doesn't take shit from anyone. "Inside I'm stronger than any of them; I have to be. I've got a really loud voice, and I'm not shy about using it. I'll fight anyone who's out to get me."

He's taken on the band office and the welfare office. He was arrested for burning down a church, then, in the absence of any evidence, immediately released. "Believe me, I've got better things to do than go around burning churches." Accused of shooting a man, Allan was targetted by the victim's brother until he convinced him he'd had nothing to do with the shooting. "They've found eleven dead bodies around the reserve. My brother and my cousin are both up for murder. This place is a mess. The people who run it don't care if we live or die."

Is this why he ran for band council? "I ran for the younger generation. People around here are tired; they're stuck in the old ways – either they're drunk or they're traditional. Then there's Rob and me." Some 1,200 people live on the Shubenacadie reserve, the majority of them under eighteen. "I thought if I lost the election I'd get out of here and never come back. But then I thought, why the hell should *I* go? Maybe in two years I'll run for band council again. *Somebody* has to do something around here."

He's fallen quiet. I wonder if he's dozed off and the interview is over – but Allan stirs again. "I don't know if I can hang around that long. I have all these dreams, you know? I'd really like to go to the

U.S, to New York, some place where I could have some fun and be myself. It's hell here; it really is. If I live to be thirty, that's not bad for this place."

▶ 54 DIFFERENT MEDICINES

"MY GRANDMOTHER WENT OUT BY HERSELF TO HUNT moose and bear. The other women would ask her, 'Aren't you scared?' She'd just laugh; she'd say, 'This is the way I've always lived, whether I have a man beside me or not.' I've heard stories of men who were very good at making clothes, or who made wonderful mocassins. And there are legends of people having different medicines. The thing that really matters is what you do with what you've got."

John is Dene. Thirty-seven, he lives in Yellowknife with his partner Robert and their housemate, Elizabeth, a teacher from Germany. The three of them bought the house together. From the upper level you can see the city on one side and an inlet of Great Slave Lake on the other. Floatplanes buzz in and out like gnats.

John's father and mother were raised in the bush, with no formal schooling in the white system. "My father wanted his kids to go to school, so in the mid-'50s they moved into Yellowknife. He got a job mining gold. My mother was very traditional in the Dene way, always sharing, always helping out and caring for the sick." She died in 1974. At seventeen John went to university in Edmonton, and for the first time became aware of racism. "On the buses, in school, even on the street I felt I wasn't supposed to be there – it was a really aggressive, bad energy." He won a scholarship to an international university in Wales. "Meeting people from so many cultures, it made me start to wonder about my own. People would ask me questions about Dene ways, but I couldn't really answer – I'd never paid much attention to how the Dene do things and see the world."

He also began to wonder about his sexuality. "From about age five I knew I was different from other boys, but I didn't really know how or why." In Wales he wondered if he might be homosexual, but left it at that. At twenty-one he came home to live with his dad for two years, in the bush. It was a crash course in Dene ways: hunting, trapping, surviving off the land, and at night, hearing the old stories. "I assumed there were no other gays in the north, and certainly none among the Dene; I had to be the only one. Now I know most of them are married." With his father pressing him not to waste his education in the bush, John went off to study languages at university, first in Québec then in Montréal. There he began the tortuous process of emerging from his sexual cocoon.

Venturing out to his first gay dance, he lingered, finally went in and watched, shaking like a leaf. A man approached, invited him to a party. John panicked, said no, and ran. At the university sports complex, a man kept looking at him. One day in the shower, "I turned around and there he was, naked. I almost fainted; I couldn't say a word. Dene people are very shy about their bodies; they don't like to expose themselves."

Eventually another man came out to him directly. "It was still very hard for me even to talk about sexuality, much less *do* anything." Three months later they had sex. "I liked how it made me feel, being with a man – not just sexually but emotionally too – and I wondered why I'd had to go through all that anguish just to get to the point where I could finally say, 'Okay, this is who I am.'" They were lovers for a year, until the other man returned to his home town.

For John and Robert, first sighting occurred in the shower at the sports complex. "I thought he looked interesting," says John, "but way too old for me." He laughs – Robert is four years older. They became friends, then roommates, but not lovers. "I felt more and more relaxed with him," says John. "I guess a lot of the negative images I still had of homosexuals were disappearing." Robert went off travelling for six months. In 1986 John got a job in Vancouver, and Robert followed him there. Then John's father invited him north for a winter of hunting and trapping. I have a friend, said John. No problem, said his father, bring him along.

Robert grew up in an anglo suburb west of Montréal. By his late teens he knew he wanted to have sex with men. "I had several brief, unsuccessful affairs with women, and the same with men." Working on oil rigs and in the merchant marine, he travelled the globe – but made no gay contacts. In the early '80s he returned to Montréal and fell in with a circle of people who ran Androgyny, a gay and lesbian book store. "Suddenly I was meeting all these openly gay men, and some of them were expressing interest in me sexually – it was an amazing and trying time for me." Then he met John.

"I liked him right away," says Robert. "But I was immersed in a political milieu that was strongly anti-monogamy. Also I was a loner, and used to being independent. But when he invited me to join his family in the bush, I thought, when would I ever have another chance like that?"

In September they flew into the camp where John's family had built two log cabins. It's on the north shore of Great Bear Lake, on the Arctic Circle. Robert: "A bear had knocked out the windows, so we had to repair them, chink the walls, and put up a one-foot layer of moss on the roof. They hunted caribou, snared rabbits, hunted ducks and fished. I wasn't much help; mostly I just watched. I was a suburban faggot, a *vegetarian*."

John laughs. "To us, caribou tongue is a luxury. We love eating the moose jaw, the brain, the intestines, and the same with fish – the guts, the eyes, the cheeks. Robert was in shock." Robert: "In November they went out on the trap lines, so for weeks I'd be alone all day. I'd do the chores – cut wood, haul and thaw water, and in the few hours the sun was above the horizon, I'd read. In the evening we'd sit around the woodstove and John's father would tell stories – of his own background, and the legends. It was amazing, unforgettable."

Back in Yellowknife – Robert assumed they were just passing through – John was offered several jobs, and this has been home ever since. In 1989 they set off on a trip to Asia. After they returned John became ill, feverish. Tests revealed TB; he was treated and he improved, but his doctor suggested he get an HIV test. In Vancouver he was told the test was positive; he had no T4 cells, dangerously low blood counts, and only a few months to live.

"I didn't believe that I would die. In my dreams my mother

started talking to me. I've come to believe she's a medicine woman, and she's teaching me how to cope with the virus. I think I'll live to be a hundred." Montréal friends keep him posted on the latest medications and treatment programs. "By now I probably know more about treating HIV than my doctor does."

A few years ago John nearly died of a lung infection. "I think I was the only one who didn't believe I was going to die." His ability to hear has been fading, making it difficult to have conversations with more than one person. "I don't go out to many social functions any more. But that's all right; I enjoy doing things at home." He's come out to his sisters, but not to his father, at least not directly. "One day I heard him say to Robert, 'You take good care of John.' I was quite moved by that. Always there's been this nagging fear that I'll be rejected by my own people. But I think as time passes it will be important to share this information about myself more and more." Robert helped get AIDS Yellowknife started.

Even as he retreats from the social realm, John's world continues to expand. "In the Dene vision, each one of us has a purpose here. We have to discover what that is, and live it as fully as we can. At this point mine is to share more of who I am and what I can do." He writes original plays for a local theatre group that re-enacts Dene legends. "In English we'd be called Winter Sun, for the long nights when the stories were told." He also writes historical material for the Northwest Territories museum, consulting with elders and medicine people. From his father's handwritten pages he's been typing a second volume of Dene legends, for publication. "Sometimes he doesn't explain things very well, so I'll ask him to enlarge on them, or to verify certain points I don't understand." He also wants to use the linguistic skills he acquired at university. "The Dene language has no manual; there's no way to teach it except by direct contact. I'd like to write something to help with that. Maybe next year."

"I really don't know what the future will bring. If I had caribou medicine I would. Did you know caribou can see the future?"

Barb

"MY ELDER'S WIFE SAID TO ME, 'IF YOU WANT TO TAKE part in a ceremony you have to wear a skirt. Women wear skirts at ceremonies.' I said, 'I understand, but I don't belong in a skirt, that's not me.' She said, 'It's a way for women to honour themselves as women, a way of balancing the male energy.' I said, 'Fine – but why do I have to wear a skirt to prove that I'm a woman?' Finally, after a long discussion, we came to a kind of agreement – for certain ceremonies, yes, I will wear a skirt, but for others I won't. Now my elder looks at me, he makes a face. I just say, 'I'm here, this is who I am.' And he says – 'Okay.'"

Barb is twenty-nine. She lives with her partner in Vernon, in British Columbia's Okanagan Valley. Growing up in small-town Alberta, she knew she wasn't like the other kids, neither boys nor girls. "I was kind of in the middle, a tomboy, and no one ever questioned that. No one in my family talked about *anything*." She didn't date boys, had crushes on girls. At fourteen she told her best friend she was gay. "*Big* mistake. The next day everyone in the school knew, everyone in the town knew – except my parents; for some reason no one told them. After that I was afraid to trust anyone." She started drinking and doing drugs, and joined the military. "It's a great way to hide, and a good place to drink. I could just go off into oblivion and forget about everything."

When she was nineteen Barb met a woman, left the military, and came out to both her divorced parents. Her father said, 'Fine, as long as you're happy,' but her mother wouldn't speak to her for two years. Other relatives attacked Barb for giving her poor mother so much grief. "It took me a long time to catch on that I hadn't done anything wrong, I was just trying to be me for a change." Her relationship ended; she kicked the chemicals. Suddenly one day her mother called. "She'd really done her homework, read a lot, and talked to a counsellor. By the time I met my present partner, things had pretty much turned around with her."

Her journey of self-discovery also took Barb back to her First Nations roots. She was born a Mohawk. When the federal legislation on status finally changed in the mid-'80s, she chose to reclaim hers. But now she would come to the circle a woman conscious of her power, and a lesbian. "Nearly all the native people I've encountered are heterosexual, and most of the elders in this area are men. When I told my elder I wanted to try some different things in the ceremonies, he said, 'No, you can't.' I said, 'Why not?' He said, 'Well, you're different.' 'What does that mean?' 'Because you are the way you are, you have a different energy.' I told him, 'Look, I understand the need to maintain traditions, but I don't see how excluding women – or a lesbian – can stand up as any kind of valid tradition.'"

The traditions clearly define roles and tasks for women and men. "The trouble is, as a lesbian I like to float in between. I love learning from the women what it means to be a medicine woman, or how to lead a sweat lodge. On the other side I want to learn from the men how to make drums and ceremonial pipes, or how to lead a medicine wheel. But the men say, 'You can't; women aren't suited for that.' I tell them, 'I can do it. At least give me the chance to show you.' It comes back to the same old thing – why do I have to prove myself, why won't you just accept me as a person?"

In Barb's experience, coming out is as difficult in the native community as anywhere else. "There was the tradition of the berdache – these were shamans, medicine people, both men and women; they were respected and honoured, but that's long gone. The same kind of ignorance and fear has been brainwashed into all of us, and it takes an awful lot of work to get over that. The trick is to find that one individual who'll listen, and to work from there. When I told one woman she said, 'There's always been a piece missing in the way I saw you, and now that I know what it is, I understand.' For me that's the first step. After that, everything else follows."

"Jessica" and "Cassie"

CASSIE'S LESBIAN AUNT INTRODUCED THEM IN THUNDER Bay. A civil servant, Cassie was transferred to Timmins, in northeast

Ontario, and Jessica is studying at the local community college to be a drug and alcohol counsellor. Each has her own apartment. We met at Cassie's place, where they spend most of their time.

When I arrived, Cassie had been scolding Jessica for leaving a message with the secretary at work. "This secretary is really nosy, and I don't want them to know any more about me than they have to. I'm always careful to call her my roommate or my girlfriend. We never say lover."

Jessica is almost as cautious at school. "If you don't come out and you try to be friends with a man, usually he gets the wrong idea. But if you *do* come out and try to be friends with a woman, she's probably going to be scared of you in case you come onto her! It's like you're damned if you do and damned if you don't." Cassie: "There's very few places you can go together and be open here. It's just too risky."

What about the shelter of a lesbian and gay circle? There's an evolving community here, a phoneline, socials, dances. The two of them hesitate, exchange a glance. Cassie: "We go to some gay events, but somehow we don't really connect there." Jessica: "I don't know why. Other people don't seem to be on the same wavelength." Cassie: "It's a small population, and it's hard to find people with the same tastes. Like the Blue Rodeo concert we just went to; no one we knew was interested." Jessica: "I find if you try to be friends with another lesbian you can easily step into somebody else's territory. There's so damn much insecurity out there."

The two of them seem out of place, on the way somewhere. How did they get here? Cassie is thirty-one. She grew up in a small town in northwest Ontario. "As a kid I was quite athletic, and people referred to me as a tomboy. I was always attracted in some way to other girls, but I repressed it; I had a heterosexual mentality – I had boyfriends. I never cooed over men like women are supposed to though; I always thought I deserved better. But it took me until a couple of years ago, when my last relationship with a man broke up, to stop lying to myself. I've never felt so close to anyone before as I do with her. It's almost like being inside her skin."

Jessica is twenty-nine. She was born on a small reserve, population, 500 or so, in northwest Ontario. "It's quite remote and no one ever heard of anything like being gay. When a girlfriend came on to me in school I pounded her – you just didn't do that; it was unheard of. I told all my other friends about her. Later when I was starting to accept it, I tried to talk with her, but it was too late, she wouldn't have anything to do with me."

By thirteen she knew she didn't fit. "I couldn't tell anyone. My family's pentecostal. I knew I had to get out of there. I wanted to go to high school." Her father refused – none of her older brothers and sisters had gone, why should she? It took a year of fighting to get her way. "By the time I finished high school I knew I was attracted to women, but I still thought it was wrong, and there was still no one I could talk to about it." She caught the bus to Toronto, found the Gay and Lesbian Counselling Centre, and began the long process of self-acceptance.

Recently the two of them went to a women's dance in Toronto. Cassie: "There must have been 400 women there; they were so free – some of them showed their bodies; they did whatever they wanted to do. Coming from a small town, I thought, wow, this must be how people feel when they go to Hollywood!" Jessica: "When I'm finished my course here, I want to get work in Toronto, as a drug and alcohol counsellor. Then I can take that experience back home with me."

After fighting so hard to get out, she wants to go back? "I'm torn. I want to live in my home community. I like being up north; it's where I belong. When I go home I get so much out of it; I'm always laughing and making people laugh – that doesn't happen in English." Her first language is a mix of Ojibway and Cree. "That's why I'm taking this course, so I can go back up there to work. But I also want to live with my lover. The way things are at home – I don't know. In Toronto I can be who I am as a lesbian, and back home I can be who I am as an Ojibway." She shrugs. "It's hard to know what to do."

And Cassie? "I'll go wherever I can find the most support, wherever it feels like home."

▶ 56 SHAMELESS IN P.E.I.

AS IN, "SHAMELESSNESS IS THE BEGINNING OF FREEDOM"
– Simone de Beauvoir.

The first time he cruised the men's rooms at the Fredericton mall, Leith Chu was fourteen. He was looking for sex with older men. "Now I think, if those men are criminals, what did that make me? I knew exactly what I was doing. I *needed* those men, and I probably used them a lot more than they ever used me. I didn't know anyone my own age who was gay or lesbian; I had no one to talk to. I needed to know about sex and being gay, and the men at the mall were my only real connection to that whole world."

This need to know has driven Leith Chu for most of his twenty-seven years. Born into a Chinese-Canadian family, he grew up in the small city of Fredericton, New Brunswick. By the time he was twelve he was stealing gay magazines from a local store. He laughs, "I won't name the store, in case they come after me. I also took books, anything to help me find out who I was." The small Chinese community in Fredericton was close and conservative. If homosexuality was acknowledged at all, it was only as a bizarre western corruption. After Leith came out to his parents, his mother refused to speak of it, and his father would make fun of him in public.

Increasingly isolated, Leith attempted suicide at fifteen and again at nineteen. By then he was at university. "Mount Allison was very homophobic. When I came out, they tried to force me out of the residence, but I wouldn't go." Being out also cost him a job. He was told to his face that he wouldn't be hired because he was gay, before New Brunswick legislation outlawed discrimination based on sexual orientation.

Now he works as a computer programmer for the federal government in Charlottetown, Prince Edward Island. He's also a steward, grievance officer, branch chairperson, and national executive member of his professional union, and serves on its committee for human rights in the workplace. At the same time he's studying for a degree in music at the university here. Why music? "I want to teach. I like kids, and I want to share my love of music with them."

I have doubts about using the term "rural" for a civil servant who lives in a downtown bachelor apartment in the capital of the province, the birthplace of the nation. "Don't worry," says Leith, "this whole island is thoroughly rural." The population of the province is about 130,000. "Most people are in the closet here, the risk of being out is just too high." P.E.I. is one of the four provinces and territories in Canada that still deny legal protection to lesbian and gay people. The provincial government sees no need for it. But things are looking up. "This summer we had our first pride parade ever – over one hundred people showed up! And the media took notice; we're definitely here."

My first impression of Leith Chu came from an article he wrote in the Halifax-based *Gaezette*, a sort of "What I Did on my Leather Vacation" piece. I was surprised at how breezy it was, how cheerful. Isn't S&M supposed to be serious, even grim? "Not at all. Like any other kind of sex, leather sex is supposed to be enjoyable. You may not actually laugh during it – in fact that'll usually kill it [he says with a laugh] – and you may even cry or scream or shout, but if you're not enjoying it on some level, you shouldn't be doing it."

Leith's impulse to S&M came early, as soon as he knew he was gay. Recently he's been looking into the origins of the desire – once again, his need to know. "My parents were loving people, but they did believe in physical punishment for children. I think some of it comes from that, and also from the fact that when I was nineteen I was raped." He speaks more slowly here, choosing his words with particular care. "A lot of the S&M is a way for me to work through all that ... to disassociate pain from damage ... to experience the cathartic potential of pain ... to recreate concepts like authority into forms that are more acceptable to me, into things that can happen only if I participate willingly in them – only if I consent. That's the difference."

The question of consent troubles me. When I was twenty-four I *consented* to a year of electric shocks, in a sad, vain attempt to undo my sexuality, which I'd been taught to regard as sick and perverse. What exactly does it mean, "consent"? "I've given that a lot of thought," says Leith. "And I believe I have enough self-awareness to know that this is an exploration I need to be doing. I know I wouldn't let anyone manipulate me or take advantage of me. That's the whole point; I'm no longer a victim of another man's power. It's the same as cruising the mall – I know what I'm doing, and I know what I want. And that's how I understand consent."

Has race affected his life as a gay man? "At times. We're not immune; there's racism in our communities just like everywhere else. Gay North American culture can be pretty narrow, without much room for minorities except as stereotypes – you know, blacks are hung, Puerto Ricans have nice asses, Asians are submissive, et cetera. If I'm in bed with someone, I'd like to think it's because they find me attractive, not because they want to see what it's like to have sex with someone who's Chinese. On the other hand, if you don't find me attractive that's fine, but the last thing I want to hear is you don't want to have sex with me *because* I'm Asian. We have to learn to refuse this kind of nonsense. Remember Nancy Reagan? Just say no."

Inside his job and out, Leith is a computer nut; he's hooked on the Internet. In fact he and his partner were introduced via e-mail: "It was an electronic romance, sex in the '90s." The man lives across the water in Amherst, Nova Scotia. They travel back and forth as their jobs permit. "For personal reasons he can't leave Nova Scotia right now, and I don't particularly want to live in Amherst, so it's hard to plan for the future. But we'll work something out."

Since his mid-teens Leith Chu has known what he wanted from life. "A career, a partner, a nice house about thirty minutes outside a major city, two Irish setters, and matching wingback chairs in front of the fire." Any changes a decade later? "I'd settle for two cats. Dogs are too time consuming for career-oriented people to handle. And I think I've gone off wingback chairs. Maybe something in a Scandinavian style?"

THE DANCE IN SUDBURY, ONTARIO, IS PACKED; THE MUSIC booms. But when Mary Mahood-Greer makes her entrance, she turns many more heads than mine. From the big stetson down through the knotted kerchief at the neck, the custom-made bib shirt, vest, chaps and cowboy boots, she might as well be John Wayne. Well, in a way she is.

"I've always loved the Duke," she says. "When I was young I thought I was *in* love with him, like a woman's supposed to love a man, 'this is the guy for me' sort of thing. Everyone thought that was sick; they assured me I'd get over it when I met the right man and got married. But since I've come out I've realized I didn't want to be *with* him, I wanted to *be* him. You know what I mean – up there on the horse?" In her bathroom there's a pencil drawing of Wayne, and in the kitchen a large poster drawn by one of Mary's sisters says, "Give 'Em Hell, Duke." "How many gay men's apartments have you gone into and there's Marilyn Monroe up on the wall, like an icon?" A few. "Well, there you go; it's the same for me with John Wayne."

The compact apartment that Mary shares with her lover, Kelly, backs onto a classic Sudbury moonscape: dark smooth rock scoured of vegetation by the sky-scraping, acid-spewing smokestacks of the nickel refineries nearby. Shadow the dog pretends to snooze in his basket, but his eyes monitor every move. Black, thin as a whippet, he'd been badly beaten before they rescued him.

Mary is forty. Born in Hamilton, Ontario, she'd always set her face to the northern bush. She graduated from college a geological technician, and in 1980 got a job hunting mineral deposits in a vast swamp north of Kirkland Lake, in northeast Ontario. "Every day it was slurp and slosh through mud and water, every day slurp, slosh, slurp, slosh. I loved every minute of it."

Growing up, Mary hated wearing dresses, hated having long hair. She admired the broad shoulders on a classmate named Kathy. She dated boys, but felt strange, off-key, out of tune. Then in the bush she had an affair with her boss. "He was married, he had no morals and didn't care, but somehow I managed to convince myself he was the man of my dreams. I guess I was that well trained."

Evenings back in the cabin they shared, she was also reading, searching. "At first I hid from women's stuff, the books and music – I actually thought Anne Murray was it! – but finally I bought *Our Bodies, Our Selves*. There was a picture in it of this woman in a motel. She was on her knees, her ass in the air, and blood was pouring out from between her legs – she was dead, from a fucked-up abortion. That was it; something turned over in me and I couldn't fake it anymore. I wanted to help women, I wanted to be with women, I was a lesbian. But first I had to help myself, and definitely not put up with any more shit from my boss."

On May 6, 1989, Mary wrote a letter to John Wayne, in her journal. "Dear Duke: Thru all my years you have been my silent heart and soul. I wanted to write to you and tell you what a wonderful day it is. But instead I feel like I have to say goodbye." Most of her John Wayne collection – books, records, movies, scrapbooks – is in storage now at her sister's.

That same day Mary wrote coming-out letters to her parents and siblings, and told her boss. "That's okay," he said, "I always knew." He went into the adjoining room, and told her to come watch him. "He was jerking off! I didn't have the power to get up and leave the cabin, but I did manage to stay in my seat, I just kept saying no, I am not interested. At the time, that was pretty good for me." Mary told the man's wife they'd been having an affair, and he fired her. She took her case to the Ontario Human Rights Commission, where it disappeared. She left the bush anyway, her back devastated by the years of heavy, awkward work.

On disability benefits, Mary found herself a place to live in Kirkland Lake. "One day some boys, they were about eighteen or so, yelled at me from across the street, 'Dyke! Muff diver!' I thought to myself, unh-hunh, this is it, this is what I've been warned about. I walked across the street, went right up to them and said, 'Hello boys, my name is Mary Mahood-Greer, and you don't have to yell out that I'm a lesbian because I already know it.' This one guy sitting up on the hood of his truck with a beer says to me, 'Wow, far out! I never met a real lesbian before. Want a beer?' 'No thanks, I don't drink. I just wanted to tell you I don't need any shit like people yelling names at me. Thank you, and have a nice day,' I said, turned around and walked away. I was wearing these old overalls, and my legs were shaking so much I was afraid they'd fall down before I got across the street!" A big, unfettered laugh bursts out of her.

At a women's event in Toronto Mary met a woman, who moved north to live with her. To locate other lesbians they put an ad in the local paper, and got three responses but no viable contacts. Then they wrote to their local health unit, offering their names to any lesbian or gay client who might want to connect. A drug and alcohol counsellor passed the letter on to a young lesbian couple, Tammy* and Kelly.

Sexually abused since she was two, Kelly had lost herself in booze and virtually any drug she could get. After nervous weeks of putting it off, finally she and Tammy went to meet Mary and her partner. Mary: "Kelly sat very still and quiet on the couch, with her eyes cast down like some kind of goddess. She would only whisper things into Tammy's ear. I thought that was so sweet." Kelly: "I certainly noticed Mary, but I was afraid to be caught staring." The two couples spent more and more time together, talking, walking in the bush, and fishing. Like shifting constellations, in due course Kelly and Mary split from their original partners and coupled.

They moved to Sudbury, a city of about 100,000, for more options. Kelly is still recovering from nearly two decades of abuse. "Once I get my life back, I can figure out what I want to do with it." Mary's gone back to school, to get a degree in social work. "It's still the same; I want to work with women. There are so many of us out there who are suffering, in so many ways. I don't know about changing the world, but you have to start somewhere."

You got that right, pilgrim.

---

* More on her in Ch 25

▶ 58 WHAT'S INSIDE

THE FRONT DOOR BANGS. CONVERSATION STOPS. A young man bops into the dining room, laden with hockey gear. It's "Francine's" son. He sees Brian and me, does a double take. Seated at the table, I face his mother and Brian faces "Anne," her lover. Quick glances fly every which way. How much does he know? My eyes slide off to the crucifix behind him. Jesus droops from a bronze cross, mounted on wood – it's hard to imagine pain like that. Francine and her son exchange a greeting in French; he clatters off to the basement. All this takes place in less than thirty seconds. Francine says, with a slight smile, "It's all right. He knows."

We're in a small town on the Acadian coast of the Gulf of St Lawrence, in New Brunswick. The main street, la rue principale, is dominated by the brooding, low-shouldered Eglise Notre Dame. Tonight the streets hum with tiny goblins and fairies, out for loot – it's Hallowe'en.

Anne is fifty-one. One of nine kids, she grew up on a farm near here, worked with the horses, ploughing and hauling hay. "I went out with boys, lots of different ones, but I always hated it, and I didn't know why." At twenty-two she married. "He was the only one that let me alone; he was more like a friend." They had two kids. "My husband treated me right, he was good to me, and I thought I loved him. I couldn't understand, why wasn't I happy? Then maybe fifteen years ago I started having dreams that I was with women. I thought, what's this, what's happening to me? If I heard somebody talking against gays, it would make me awfully mad; I'd tell them off. It got me thinking, maybe that's it, maybe that's why I'm so unhappy. But I never had anyone to talk to. I thought I was the only one."

One night she was out in her car. "I was really desperate. So I went for a tree, with my car. I don't know – suddenly I thought of my daughter and I jammed on the brake. That's when I said to God, 'This has to stop – look, either you change my life or you come and get me.'" There's pain in her face, years of it.

Francine is forty, the youngest of eleven. When she was eight or nine, she noticed strong feelings for other girls. At fourteen, an older sister told her not to worry, it would pass. She met a boy; they dated for five years, then married. "I thought, that's it, it's like my sister said." But the feelings didn't go away. They had two children. Still the feelings didn't go away. "It would just come up, out of the blue, maybe from something I saw on TV."

As the years passed, the feelings intensified. "In my thirties I started to think, is this how it's going to be the rest of my life? I wanted to test it, to see if I really was gay or not, but being a Christian I didn't want to do anything to harm my family – my kids were twelve and thirteen by then, and my husband was an alcoholic – so I just kept still."

Four years ago Francine's father died. "I have a strong faith, so I prayed to my father to intercede for me with God. I said, 'Either change my life, or come and get me.' Within a month I was talking to this friend; I was ninety percent sure she was gay. I told her I really wanted to meet someone, another woman – not for a sexual experience but just to talk, to get things off my chest." Only days before, having just left her marriage after twenty-six years, Anne happened to have told this same friend precisely the same thing. Francine: "I'm sure that happened through God." Anne: "Me too; I'm sure of it."

Their mutual friend introduced them. They met for breakfast, talked about kids and husbands – Francine was still with hers, what was she to do? They talked about music – they both play guitar and sing – and about their feelings, so long denied. They met again, and again. Anne: "Music was the excuse we made to our families; we play for the old folks." Acadian history – the expulsion, the wandering, the struggle for place – is passed on through the music. In the front room Francine and Anne keep an array of guitars and mandolins.

Francine: "With eleven years difference between us, Anne couldn't believe I'd be interested in her. On our second date, at a restaurant, she pointed at this cute young waitress, she said, 'How would you like to have that in your bed?' I said 'No thanks, I have to know what's inside.'" Anne: "That's probably when I fell in love." They both laugh.

It's two years they've been together now. As she's done for more than twenty years, Anne still works part-time at the lobster packing plant up the coast, and in the winter at a local nursing home. Work at the plant is cold, hard on the back, low-waged, and far from secure. Anne: "The lobsters are getting smaller all the time; it means they're overfishing." Francine: "The government gives out too many trapping licences. They're going to kill it like they did the cod."

Francine is studying small business at the regional college. She plans to turn her house into a home for seniors. "With government cutbacks, there's a growing demand for that here. Unless you're very sick, there's no place to go when you're old." Anne: "We want people to feel like it's their own home." Anne will quit her jobs, and the two of them will share the work.

How are things between them and their various families? Francine: "When Anne first moved in, my son didn't like it much – he wanted her out." Anne adds, "But he's never said anything; he's always been nice to me." Francine: "Time heals." When Anne told her mother, she responded, "'It can't be, you must be crazy!' I tried and my sisters even tried to explain things to her, but she'll never accept, she's too old." Francine adds, "But she's nice to me – she doesn't show what she's thinking." At seventy-nine, Francine's mother told her a week ago that she'd met a man. "She was all excited, so that opened a door for me. I told her I'd met someone too, but it wasn't a man. She was quite surprised, but finally she said, 'If this is what makes you happy then it's okay with me.'"

I've seen two crucifixes in the house, another in the car. How do these women of faith feel about their church? Anne: "We go to church in Moncton, not here. Everyone knows us here, especially the priest." Francine: "The priest told my husband I could be cured. But I don't want to be cured. Anyway, I don't go to church for the priest, I go for God." Anne: "He talks to me in my heart, so that's what I listen to, my heart."

When they first wrote to me, offering to tell their stories, Francine and Anne said they hoped to help others in similar circumstances. I compliment them on their quiet courage and integrity. They both look a little embarrassed.

Anne says, "It's hard to come out, that's for sure. But for me it's nothing compared to what it was like before. This last year is worth all the twenty-six years I was married. If I died tomorrow, I would die happy."

▶ 59 OUR TIME

RICK POTTS CAREFULLY SEPARATES COLOURS FROM whites. He loads several machines, feeds them quarters, and then we sit and talk in a tiny laundromat in Temagami, northeast Ontario. To get here, Rick borrowed a truck and drove an hour across the ice. It's early March. After the coldest winter in decades, the ice on the lake is still strong.

Rick is thirty-one. He lives on Bear Island, a First Nations reserve in Lake Temagami. His father was Cree, his mother Irish. In the '40s they met at a swanky lodge here, she working in the kitchen, he as a fishing guide. "My dad drank, so my mom left him; she took me with her to live in North Bay. I was the only one of the six kids who didn't grow up on Bear Island."

Rick went to Catholic boarding school, first in North Bay, then in London. "In grades five and six I was most comfortable playing and skipping rope with the girls – none of my friends seemed to think that was strange. But suddenly in grade seven I began to feel a pressure to conform, to identify with the other boys. I started dressing differently, talking differently; I started to clam up and be less outgoing. Looking back, it seems to me I was shutting down my female side."

On summer vacation at Bear Island, ten-year-old Rick was looking at a straight porn magazine with a younger male relative – "I won't identify him any more than that; he's still around – and the other boy said, 'Do you want to do it?' I said, 'Do what?'" He laughs; it's a warm memory. "We gave each other head. It felt really good. I guess part of the excitement was doing something like that without getting caught."

He did well in school, but not at university. "I didn't even know why I was there, and I was much more interested in exploring the gay baths and clubs in London." Then he moved to the big city, Toronto.

"I'd go to work, come home, take a nap, eat something, have a few drinks with friends, go out to the bar round eleven, drink some more, smoke dope, do acid or coke – that was my life, that and going to the baths. I used to only fuck, but one summer here on the lake I lost my virginity, so to speak. It was nice; I enjoyed it. No condom. Back then people in the city were just starting to talk about AIDS, but there wasn't much information – and I didn't care, I never believed I could get it. Not me."

We're sitting in the dark blue Chevy half-ton, in the middle of a bay, on the ice. Even with the windows open, an unclouded sun warms the cab. We're eating Chinese food from the take-out in town. "Ethnic cleansing," says Rick, "that's what happened to me, in a way. Growing up in an all-white, Catholic milieu, I learned to be ashamed of being aboriginal. In high school I'd tell people I came from a wealthy family who owned a lodge up north. I wanted to dress myself up in someone else's identity." After university Rick got a job as a policy analyst at the Chiefs of Ontario office in Toronto. He worked awhile for a trucking company, and joined the board of a newly formed group, Two-Spirited Peoples of the First Nations. "At first I felt like an outsider – I *was* an outsider – I didn't get the jokes, half the time I didn't have a clue what people were talking about. But I'd ask questions, and I'd listen – I learned a lot by listening."

The concept of two-spiritedness was new to Rick. "If we're trying to define our own identity, the gay and lesbian labels don't fit very well, both words being derived from European languages. We know that before the Europeans came, there was a respected place in aboriginal communities for two-spirited men and women; we used to be healers and advisers. The way I understand it, 'two-spirited' means people whose male and female energies are more in balance than they might be in a heterosexual person."

In 1988 Rick tested positive for HIV. "I went into shock. I didn't want any information about the disease, no healing plans, nothing. I just smoked dope. In fact my use of drugs actually increased – at that point I didn't want to feel anything. I was only twenty-four, and I was going to die."

He quit his job with the trucking company, and went to work for the Ontario Federation of Native Friendship Centres. For the first time he was exposed to the traditions, the spiritual realm, of aboriginal life. "I met really strong people who weren't using drugs. I was still partying myself. But in May I signed up for this workshop, and one of the teachings is that in order to receive anything you have to sacrifice something, so I thought, okay, I won't smoke for three days. When the elders got talking about their journeys – how they'd got free of alcohol and the openings it created for them – I thought, that's *me* they're talking about. I started to cry. It's the first time I ever cried in public. I haven't drunk or smoked since." He cries now, just tears, no sound.

Removed a little from the downtown dance, Rick began to dream. "I started having all these amazing dreams about the community here, about old people, people who'd died, about the land, and the water – all of it was very alive, very inviting. Then one time when I was up here I dreamed of a train station, and this beautiful train made of glass, very flashy and high-tech. I knew it was waiting to take me back to Toronto. But I said no, still in the dream I said no, I need to stay here and heal." Awake, he stayed.

This is a turbulent time in Bear Island history. There are only 3,200 people on the lake, a hundred or so on the island. They've been struggling for years to regain control of their own land. And the community is divided over the issue of logging in the ancient Temagami forest. "I don't think it's coincidental that I and others have been drawn back here right now. These are people who in another generation might have chosen to be in the city, making lots of money, but instead they're here. We have gifts to offer, and we've chosen to bring them back to our own people." Last week Rick chaired a community meeting. The chief, who also happens to be his niece and best friend here, asked him to do an opening ceremony, the first he's ever done. "I was incredibly nervous. But I was honoured too, that she trusted me to do that." Tonight he'll DJ a dance on the island, after the snow-pitch tournament – that's softball on snowshoes.

Rick lives by himself in a small apartment, in someone else's house on the island. He has no vehicle, no phone. He knows of only one other two-spirited person here, a man, in the closet, a heavy drinker – they haven't spoken. When Rick refers to his community, to what degree does that include him, as a two-spirited man? "It's been hard, but I think it's starting to change. I can talk to some of my family now, about some of my feelings." Rick's family on the island is large, many branched. "I have the chance to be a role model to my nieces and nephews. They know I've been where they are now, drinking and doing drugs. And they don't see me the same way they would a parent. I'm close to their age, so I'm more like a friend or an uncle – that's an honoured role for a two-spirited person."

What about other people on the island? "A few seem to feel comfortable enough to talk with me about it. There's even a few I can joke with, like I'll say, 'I'm in the market for a man who'll come and chop wood and haul water for me; got any leads?' If anyone has a problem with it, they haven't said anything to my face, and I'm certainly not ostracized in any way. It's slow. But I have time.

"One day I put some tobacco down, as an offering to the Creator, and I said, 'Thank you for my life. But I've spent it, I've already used it up. Now I offer myself to you; my life is in your hands.' Maybe it was just bargaining, you know, a desperate grab for time? But in another way it makes perfect sense, because the life I'm living now is the best time I've ever known."

In another couple of weeks the ice will have cracked, and in a month it will have melted into the lake. The circle keeps turning.

Rick: "It's my belief that many of the ceremonies and teachings of two-spirited people went underground when the Europeans came. We were the first to go; there was no place for us in that system. I think the time is coming when we can start recovering some of those traditions – they're not dead, they're underground, in hiding. But as long as we're partying our face off in the city, there's no way we can be open to the teachings. I want to build a camp, a substance-free place where two-spirited people, including people like myself with HIV, can come together and start on the healing path.

"Our time is coming, I'm sure of it. And if I'm lucky, maybe I'll still be around to see it."

60 WINTER, AGAIN

A NEIGHBOUR TOLD US YOU CAN PREDICT HOW MUCH snow to expect by the height at which the paper wasps build their nests. In November I spotted a big one, way up near the crown of a thirty-foot elm. The snow did come early this year, blanketing the last of the carrots and beets. And it stayed, clumping on the cedars, skim milk sun pooling in the spaces between.

In the fall a new restaurant opened out our way. We dropped in for dinner. The woman who waited on us turned out to be one of the owners. She called us "Gents," making me giggle.

In two visits Brian and I had established that we live together, and learned that she and her partner (as yet unseen, gender to be determined) share a house not far from the restaurant. She said they planned to get some musicians in. "Like who?" I asked, "kd lang?" Testing, testing. She didn't miss a beat. "If kd lang was in our restaurant, believe me, it would be a private party. A *very* private party." She grinned, and went off to deliver some drinks. So.

We dropped in for their first Sunday brunch. This time the other partner was waiting tables. When she brought our coffee she said, leaning closer, "Second Saturday this month we're going to close the restaurant early and hold a special party." "Special?" I inquired, my eyebrows chasing my receding hairline. "You know," she said, "a *rainbow* party. With live music. We'll put up curtains on the front windows – that's the only way some folks will come." "Hallelujah," said I. "Will it be formal dress – long gloves, big hats?" "Check your drag bag," she replied, "I'm sure you'll find something."

For two years I've wandered this country looking for rural us, and what turns up right here in our own backyard? A couple of lesbians, big as life and all set to throw a rainbow party, everyone welcome, just so long as you're in the loop. Far as I know, this is a first for our little corner of the world. These women are making history.

But – a *party*? Oh my God. It's been so long. What to wear? What to say? What dances are they doing these days? How many people will be there? I want no more than a handful, so as not to be over-whelmed; Brian wants as many as the place can hold, so as not to stand out.

Maybe there'll be a blizzard that night, and we won't be able to get down the hill.

Saturday night. We've showered, brushed our hair (some of us have gelled it, too), and put on clean clothes. It's time to go. But Brian is caught up in a Doris Day/Rock Hudson movie on the telly. I'm sitting at the big window in the bathroom, mesmerized by the winter's first serious blizzard. Tonight, of all nights. With the yard light on, it's a breath-taking show. Schools of tiny white fish dart through black water. Clouds of smoke swirl off the roof. Photons float suspended for an instant – a light year? – then blur into infinity. Such exuberant, effortless beauty, how can it be?

There'll be other parties.

Before I met Brian, I had no idea that human interaction could be so intimate so easily. Not that we haven't worked at it. By now we've tuned our coupling to such a fine degree of mutual respect and delight, the temptation is overwhelming to stay home where it's warm, safe, and we know the language. It's a cozy nest we've built for ourselves. Cozy, and very small. The tyrants have us exactly where they want us – isolated, out of the fray, and, against all our better instincts, a little nuclear unit, thoroughly privatized.

It is well after our usual bedtime when we leave the house, and set our faces into the storm.

Ordering Information

Out Our Way: Gay and Lesbian Life in the Country
is available through bookstores or directly from the publisher.

To order from the publisher, please send $24.56 (includes shipping and GST) by cheque, money order, or VISA (send complete card information including expiry date) with your mailing address to Between The Lines, 720 Bathurst St., #404, Toronto, Ont. M5S 2R4.

A complete catalogue of our titles is also available by request.